CEOE Field 10 OSAT
Biological Sciences
Teacher Certification Exam

By: Sharon Wynne, M.S
Southern Connecticut State University

"And, while there's no reason yet to panic, I think it's only prudent that we make preparations to panic."

XAMonline, INC.
Boston

Copyright © 2007 XAMonline, Inc.

All rights reserved. No part of the material protected by this copyright notice may be reproduced or utilized in any form or by any means, electronic or mechanical, including photocopying, recording or by any information storage and retrievable system, without written permission from the copyright holder.

To obtain permission(s) to use the material from this work for any purpose including workshops or seminars, please submit a written request to:

XAMonline, Inc.
21 Orient Ave.
Melrose, MA 02176
Toll Free 1-800-301-4647
Email: info@xamonline.com
Web www.xamonline.com
Fax: 1-781-662-9268

Library of Congress Cataloging-in-Publication Data

Wynne, Sharon A.
    OSAT Biological Sciences Field 10: Teacher Certification / Sharon A. Wynne. -2nd ed.
    ISBN 978-1-58197-780-6
    1. OSAT Biological Sciences Field 10.   2. Study Guides.   3. CEOE
    4. Teachers' Certification & Licensure.   5. Careers

Disclaimer:

The opinions expressed in this publication are the sole works of XAMonline and were created independently from the National Education Association, Educational Testing Service, or any State Department of Education, National Evaluation Systems or other testing affiliates.

Between the time of publication and printing, state specific standards as well as testing formats and website information may change that is not included in part or in whole within this product. Sample test questions are developed by XAMonline and reflect similar content as on real tests; however, they are not former tests. XAMonline assembles content that aligns with state standards but makes no claims nor guarantees teacher candidates a passing score. Numerical scores are determined by testing companies such as NES or ETS and then are compared with individual state standards. A passing score varies from state to state.

Printed in the United States of America

CEOE: OSAT Biological Sciences Field 10
ISBN: 978-1-58197-780-6

TEACHER CERTIFICATION STUDY GUIDE

TABLE OF CONTENTS   PG

SUBAREA I—FOUNDATIONS OF SCIENTIFIC INQUIRY

Competency 0001 - Understand common themes among the sciences and the relationships that connect mathematics, technology, and science 1

     Skill 1.1 Similarities among systems in math, science, and technology 1

     Skill 1.2 Apply concepts and theories from mathematics and other sciences to a biological system 1

     Skill 1.3 Analyze the use of biology and other sciences in the design of a technological solution to a given problem 2

     Skill 1.4 Use a variety of software and information technologies (e.g., spreadsheets, graphing utilities, statistical packages, simulations, on-line resources) to model and solve problems in mathematics, science, and technology 3

Competency 0002 - Understand the historical and contemporary contexts of biological study and the applications of biology and biotechnology to everyday life 4

     Skill 2.1 Analyze the significance of key events in the history of biological study 4

     Skill 2.2 Assess the societal implications of recent developments in biology and biotechnology 5

Competency 0003 - Understand the process of scientific inquiry and the role of observation, experimentation, and communication in explaining natural phenomena 7

     Skill 3.1 Processes by which scientific knowledge and hypotheses are generated and revised 7

     Skill 3.2 Analyze ethical practices related to the process of scientific research and reporting 7

     Skill 3.3 Evaluate the appropriateness of a specified experimental design to test a hypothesis 9

     Skill 3.4 Analyze the use of models in explaining and investigating natural phenomena 9

TEACHER CERTIFICATION STUDY GUIDE

Competency 0004 - Understand principles of measurement and the processes of gathering, interpreting, and communicating scientific data 11

    Skill 4.1 Evaluate the appropriateness of a given method or procedure for collecting data for a specified purpose 11

    Skill 4.2 Evaluate the appropriateness and limitations of units of measurement, measuring devices, or methods of measurement 11

    Skill 4.3 Knowledge of appropriate and effective graphic representation of Data 11

    Skill 4.4 Select an effective graphic representation (e.g., graph, table, diagram) for organizing, reporting, and analyzing given experimental data 12

Competency 0005 - Understand the use of equipment, materials, chemicals, and organisms used in biological studies and the application of procedures for their proper, safe, and legal use 14

    Skill 5.1 Demonstrate knowledge of the appropriate use of laboratory instruments and equipment 14

    Skill 5.2 Storing, identifying, and disposing of chemicals and biological materials 15

    Skill 5.3 Use of live specimens 16

    Skill 5.4 Dissection and alternatives to dissection 17

    Skill 5.5 Laboratory Safety Procedures 17

SUBAREA II—CELL STRUCTURE AND FUNCTION

Competency 0006 - Understand the functions and interrelatedness of cell structures, and identify the structural features of different types of cells 19

    Skill 6.1 Compare prokaryotes and eukaryotes 19

    Skill 6.2 Understand the importance of active and passive transport 22

Competency 0007 - Understand basic chemistry and biochemistry, and use this understanding to analyze the role of biologically important elements and compounds in living organisms 26

    Skill 7.1 Compare and contrast hydrogen, ionic, and covalent bonds 26

Skill 7.2 Analyze the structure and function of carbohydrates, lipids, proteins, and nucleic acids 27

Skill 7.3 Analyze the properties of water and its significance to living organisms 30

Skill 7.4 Analyze the structure and function of enzymes and factors 31

Competency 0008 - Understand the processes of photosynthesis and cellular respiration and their relationships to cell structure and function 33

Skill 8.1 Analyze limiting factors that affect the yield of energy from the breakdown of organic molecules in a cell 33

Skill 8.2 Understand the significance of photosynthesis and respiration to living organisms 34

Skill 8.3 Evaluate the significance of chloroplast structure and mitochondrion structure in the processes of photosynthesis and respiration 38

Skill 8.4 Compare C3 and C4 photosynthesis 39

Competency 0009 - Understand the structure and function of DNA and RNA 40

Skill 9.1 DNA replication, potential errors, and implications of these errors 40

Skill 9.2 Protein Synthesis 42

Skill 9.3 Mutations in DNA molecules and their effect on protein structure and function 43

Skill 9.4 Control of gene expression in cells 44

SUBAREA III—HEREDITY AND BIOLOGICAL ADAPTATION

Competency 0010 - Understand the procedures involved in the isolation, manipulation, and expression of genetic material and the application of genetic engineering in basic and applied research 46

Skill 10.1 Understand the role of genetic engineering in the medical field 46

Skill 10.2 Knowledge of genetic engineering techniques 47

Competency 0011 - Understand the cell cycle, the stages and end products of meiosis and mitosis, and the role of cell division in unicellular and multicellular organisms 48

    Skill 11.1 Knowledge of cell division 48

    Skill 11.2 Understand genetic diversity 52

    Skill 11.3 Understand the relationship between an unrestricted cell cycle and cancer 52

Competency 0012 - Understand concepts, principles, and applications of classical and molecular genetics 53

    Skill 12.1 Understand the basic principle of heredity 53

    Skill 12.2 Analyze genetic inheritance problems......................................55

    Skill 12.3 Analyze the techniques used to screen for genetic disorders 56

    Skill 12.4 Understand the role of nonnuclear inheritance 57

Competency 0013 - Understand the principles of population genetics and the interaction between heredity and the environment, and apply this knowledge to problems involving populations 58

    Skill 13.1 Analyze the conditions that affect the gene pool 58

    Skill 13.2 Recognize the relationship between phenotype and its selective advantage in the environment 59

Competency 0014 - Understand the processes of natural selection and adaptation and evolutionary theory 60

    Skill 14.1 Analyze the role of natural selection on evolution 60

    Skill 14.2 Compare alternative mechanisms of evolution 60

    Skill 14.3 Recognize the factors that lead to speciation...........................61

    Skill 14.4 Evaluate observations made in various areas of biology (e.g., embryology, biochemistry, anatomy) in terms of evolutionary theory 62

TEACHER CERTIFICATION STUDY GUIDE

SUBAREA IV—MATTER, ENERGY, AND ORGANIZATION IN ORGANISMS

Competency 0015 - Understand the principles of taxonomy 64

    Skill 15.1 Knowledge of the classification of organisms 64

    Skill 15.2 Analyzing a phylogenetic tree or cladogram of related species ... 65

    Skill 15.3 Analyzing the impact of evolution and modern genetics in the classification system 65

    Skill 15.4 Recognize the functions of specialized structures at all levels of complexity (e.g., leaves on trees, wings on birds) 65

Competency 0016 - Understand the unity and diversity of life, including common structures and functions 66

    Skill 16.1 Knowledge of the properties of life 66

    Skill 16.2 Recognize the level of organization 66

    Skill 16.3 Comparing and analyzing the basic life functions carried out by living organisms (e.g., obtaining nutrients, excretion, reproduction) 66

    Skill 16.4 Recognize the importance of maintaining biological diversity (e.g., pharmacological products, stability of ecosystems) 68

    Skill 16.5 Analyze the processes involved in homeostasis 69

Competency 0017 - Understand the characteristics, functions, and adaptations of viruses, archaebacteria, monerans, protoctists (protists), and fungi 70

    Skill 17.1 Analyze the structure and processes of prions and viruses 70

    Skill 17.2 Compare archaebacteria and eubacteria 70

    Skill 17.3 Chromosome and plasmid replication in bacteria 71

    Skill 17.4 Structure and function of protists 72

    Skill 17.5 Knowledge of the significance of fungi, bacteria, and viruses 72

    Skill 17.6 Analyze the process of gene transfer in monerans 73

BIOLOGICAL SCIENCES

Competency 0018 - Understand the characteristics, functions, and adaptations of plants 74

    Skill 18.1 Features of plants 74

    Skill 18.2 Reproduction and development of plants....................................... 75

    Skill 18.3 Knowledge of transport in plants.. 76

    Skill 18.4 Evaluate the adaptive significance of plant structures (e.g., sporangia, microphylls, modified leaves, colorful flowers)........................... 76

Competency 0019 - Understand the characteristics, functions, and adaptations of animals 78

    Skill 19.1 Identify the general characteristics of vertebrate and invertebrate development.. 78

    Skill 19.2 Knowledge of physiological processes of animals 79

    Skill 19.3 Predict relative metabolic rates of animals (e.g., endotherms, ectotherms, animals of different sizes) 89

    Skill 19.4 Analyze the importance of animal behaviors................................ 80

SUBAREA V—INTERDEPENDENCE OF ORGANISMS

Competency 0020 - Understand the structures and functions of the human skeletal, muscular, and integumentary systems; common malfunctions of these systems; and their homeostatic relationships within the body................................ 81

    Skill 20.1 Structures, locations, and functions of the three types of muscular tissue 81

    Skill 20.2 Understand the mechanism of skeletal muscular contraction 81

    Skill 20.3 Analyze the movements of body joints... 81

    Skill 20.4 Knowledge of the structure and function of skin.......................... 82

    Skill 20.5 Demonstrate an understanding of possible causes and effects of malfunctions of the skeletal, muscular, and integumentary systems (e.g., arthritis, skin cancer).. 82

TEACHER CERTIFICATION STUDY GUIDE

Competency 0021 - Understand the structures and functions of the human respiratory and excretory systems, common malfunctions of these systems, and their homeostatic relationships within the body...85

    Skill 21.1 Surface area, volume, and function of the respiratory and excretory systems 85

    Skill 21.2 Knowledge of process of breathing and gas exchange................85

    Skill 21.3 Analyze factors that influence the characteristics of the major types of biomes Knowledge of osmoregulation and waste removal.............86

    Skill 21.4 Recognize the effect of biome degradation and destruction on biosphere stability (e.g., climate changes, deforestation, reduction of species diversity)Malfunctions of the respiratory and excretory systems.....87

Competency 0022 - Understand the structures and functions of the human circulatory and immune systems, common malfunctions of these systems, and their homeostatic relationships within the body..88

    Skill 22.1 Analyze the structure, function, and regulation of the heart 88

    Skill 22.2 Malfunctions of the circulatory system 89

    Skill 22.3 Structure, function, and regulation of the immune system 89

    Skill 22.4 Malfunctions of the immune system...91

Competency 0023 - Understand human nutrition and the structures and functions of the human digestive system and accessory organs, common malfunctions of the digestive system, and its homeostatic relationships within the body 92

    Skill 23.1 Understand the roles of basic nutrients found in foods 92

    Skill 23.2 Understand the mechanisms of digestion and indigestion 92

    Skill 23.3 Malfunctions of the digestive system..93

Competency 0024 - Understand the structures and functions of the human nervous and endocrine systems, common malfunctions of these systems, and their homeostatic relationships within the body...94

    Skill 24.1 Knowledge of the central and peripheral nervous systems 94

Skill 24.2 Analyze the role of nerve impulses and neurons 94

Skill 24.3 Discuss the influence of drugs and other chemicals on nerve transmission 95

Skill 24.4 Understand the feedback mechanisms in homeostasis 96

Skill 24.5 Malfunctions of the nervous and endocrine systems 96

Competency 0025 - Understand the structures and functions of the human reproductive systems, their homeostatic relationships within the body, processes of embryonic development, common malfunctions of the reproductive systems, and sexually transmitted diseases 97

    Skill 25.1 Understand the major endocrine glands and the function of their hormones 97

    Skill 25.2 Understand hormone control and development and function of male and female reproductive systems 97

    Skill 25.3 Gametogenesis, fertilization, and birth control 98

    Skill 25.4 Embryonic and fetal development 99

    Skill 25.5 Potential effects of drugs, alcohol, and nutrition on fetal development 99

    Skill 25.6 Malfunctions of the reproductive systems (e.g., infertility, birth defects) 100

    Skill 25.7 Demonstrate an understanding of sexually transmitted diseases 101

Competency 0026 - Understand the characteristics of populations and communities, and use this knowledge to analyze population growth and community interactions 103

    Skill 26.1 Factors that affect population size and growth rate 103

    Skill 26.2 Population growth curves 103

    Skill 26.3 Relationships among organisms in a community 104

Competency 0027 - Understand the development and structure of ecosystems and the characteristics of major biomes.. 106

    Skill 27.1 Flow of energy through trophic levels of an ecosystem 106

    Skill 27.2 Pyramid models 107

    Skill 27.3 Ecological succession and biotic and abiotic factors........................... 107

Competency 0028 - Understand the connections within and among the biogeochemical cycles, and analyze their implications for living things 109

    Skill 28.1 Recognize the importance of the processes involved in the water cycle 109

    Skill 28.2 Role of decomposers in nutrient cycling... 109

    Skill 28.3 Analyze the role of respiration and photosynthesis in biogeochemical cycling 109

    Skill 28.4 Evaluate the effects of limiting factors on ecosystem productivity (e.g., light intensity, gas concentrations, mineral availability)....................... 111

Competency 0029 - Understand concepts of human ecology and the impact of human decisions and activities on the abiotic and biotic environments 112

    Skill 29.1 Recognize the importance and implications of influencing factors (e.g., nutrition, public health) on human population dynamics 112

    Skill 29.2 Predict the impact of human use of natural resources (e.g., forests, rivers) on organisms.. 112

    Skill 29.3 Analyze types of resource misuse and their long- and short-term effects 113

    Skill 29.4 Evaluate methods and technologies that reduce or mitigate environmental degradation 113

Sample Test..115

Answer Key 136

Rationales for Sample Questions 137

TEACHER CERTIFICATION STUDY GUIDE

Great Study and Testing Tips!

What to study in order to prepare for the subject assessments is the focus of this study guide but equally important is *how* you study.

You can increase your chances of truly mastering the information by taking some simple, but effective steps.

Study Tips:

1. Some foods aid the learning process. Foods such as milk, nuts, seeds, rice, and oats help your study efforts by releasing natural memory enhancers called CCKs (*cholecystokinin*) composed of *tryptopha*n, *choline*, and *phenylalanine*. All of these chemicals enhance the neurotransmitters associated with memory. Before studying, try a light, protein-rich meal of eggs, turkey, and fish. All of these foods release the memory enhancing chemicals. The better the connections, the more you comprehend.

Likewise, before you take a test, stick to a light snack of energy boosting and relaxing foods. A glass of milk, a piece of fruit, or some peanuts all release various memory-boosting chemicals and help you to relax and focus on the subject at hand.

2. Learn to take great notes. A by-product of our modern culture is that we have grown accustomed to getting our information in short doses (i.e. TV news sound bites or USA Today style newspaper articles.)

Consequently, we've subconsciously trained ourselves to assimilate information better in neat little packages. If your notes are scrawled all over the paper, it fragments the flow of the information. Strive for clarity. Newspapers use a standard format to achieve clarity. Your notes can be much clearer through use of proper formatting. A very effective format is called *"Cornell Method."*

> Take a sheet of loose-leaf lined notebook paper and draw a line all the way down the paper about 1-2" from the left-hand edge.
>
> Draw another line across the width of the paper about 1-2" up from the bottom. Repeat this process on the reverse side of the page.

Look at the highly effective result. You have ample room for notes, a left hand margin for special emphasis items or inserting supplementary data from the textbook, a large area at the bottom for a brief summary, and a little rectangular space for just about anything you want.

BIOLOGICAL SCIENCES

3. **Get the concept then the details.** Too often we focus on the details and don't gather an understanding of the concept. However, if you simply memorize only dates, places, or names, you may well miss the whole point of the subject.

A key way to understand things is to put them in your own words. If you are working from a textbook, automatically summarize each paragraph in your mind. If you are outlining text, don't simply copy the author's words.

Rephrase them in your own words. You remember your own thoughts and words much better than someone else's, and subconsciously tend to associate the important details to the core concepts.

4. **Ask Why?** Pull apart written material paragraph by paragraph and don't forget the captions under the illustrations.

Example: If the heading is "Stream Erosion", flip it around to read "Why do streams erode?" Then answer the questions.

If you train your mind to think in a series of questions and answers, not only will you learn more, but it also helps to lessen the test anxiety because you are used to answering questions.

5. **Read for reinforcement and future needs.** Even if you only have 10 minutes, put your notes or a book in your hand. Your mind is similar to a computer; you have to input data in order to have it processed. *By reading, you are creating the neural connections for future retrieval.* The more times you read something, the more you reinforce the learning of ideas.

Even if you don't fully understand something on the first pass, *your mind stores much of the material for later recall.*

6. **Relax to learn so go into exile.** Our bodies respond to an inner clock called biorhythms. Burning the midnight oil works well for some people, but not everyone.

If possible, set aside a particular place to study that is free of distractions. Shut off the television, cell phone, and pager and exile your friends and family during your study period.

If you really are bothered by silence, try background music. Light classical music at a low volume has been shown to aid in concentration over other types. Music that evokes pleasant emotions without lyrics is highly suggested. Try just about anything by Mozart. It relaxes you.

BIOLOGICAL SCIENCES

7. Use arrows not highlighters. At best, it's difficult to read a page full of yellow, pink, blue, and green streaks. Try staring at a neon sign for a while and you'll soon see that the horde of colors obscure the message.

A quick note, a brief dash of color, an underline, and an arrow pointing to a particular passage is much clearer than a horde of highlighted words.

8. Budget your study time. Although you shouldn't ignore any of the material, *allocate your available study time in the same ratio that topics may appear on the test.*

Testing Tips:

1. Get smart, play dumb. Don't read anything into the question. Don't make an assumption that the test writer is looking for something else than what is asked. Stick to the question as written and don't read extra things into it.

2. Read the question and all the choices *twice* before answering the question. You may miss something by not carefully reading, and then re-reading both the question and the answers.

If you really don't have a clue as to the right answer, leave it blank on the first time through. Go on to the other questions, as they may provide a clue as to how to answer the skipped questions.

If later on, you still can't answer the skipped ones . . . *Guess.* The only penalty for guessing is that you *might* get it wrong. Only one thing is certain; if you don't put anything down, you will get it wrong!

3. Turn the question into a statement. Look at the way the questions are worded. The syntax of the question usually provides a clue. Does it seem more familiar as a statement rather than as a question? Does it sound strange?

By turning a question into a statement, you may be able to spot if an answer sounds right, and it may also trigger memories of material you have read.

4. Look for hidden clues. It's actually very difficult to compose multiple-foil (choice) questions without giving away part of the answer in the options presented.

In most multiple-choice questions you can often readily eliminate one or two of the potential answers. This leaves you with only two real possibilities and automatically your odds go to Fifty-Fifty for very little work.

5. Trust your instincts. For every fact that you have read, you subconsciously retain something of that knowledge. On questions that you aren't really certain about, go with your basic instincts. **Your first impression on how to answer a question is usually correct.**

6. Mark your answers directly on the test booklet. Don't bother trying to fill in the optical scan sheet on the first pass through the test.

Just be very careful not to miss-mark your answers when you eventually transcribe them to the scan sheet.

7. Watch the clock! You have a set amount of time to answer the questions. Don't get bogged down trying to answer a single question at the expense of 10 questions you can more readily answer.

THIS PAGE BLANK

SUBAREA I—FOUNDATIONS OF SCIENTIFIC INQUIRY

Competency 0001 Understand common themes among the sciences and the relationships that connect mathematics, technology, and science.

Skill 1.1 Similarities among systems in math, science, and technology.

Math, science, and technology have common themes in how they are applied and understood. All three use **models**, **diagrams**, and **graphs** to simplify a concept for analysis and interpretation. **Patterns** observed in these systems lead to predictions based on these observations. Another common theme among these three systems is equilibrium. **Equilibrium** is a state in which forces are balanced, resulting in **stability**. Static equilibrium is stability due to a lack of changes and dynamic equilibrium is stability due to a balance between opposite forces. **Scale** is a ratio of size. For example, a map may have a scale of true miles per every inch drawn on the map. A model drawn to scale is a representation of something that is larger or smaller than its actual size. There is also the very literal interpretation of scale. In this context the scale would be used to measure mass, and would often be called a balance.

Skill 1.2 Apply concepts and theories from mathematics and other sciences to a biological system.

The knowledge and use of basic mathematical concepts and skills is a necessary aspect of scientific study. Science depends on data and the manipulation of data requires knowledge of mathematics. Understanding of basic statistics, graphs and charts, and algebra are of particular importance. Scientists must be able to understand and apply the statistical concepts of mean, median, mode, and range to sets of scientific data. In addition, scientists must be able to represent data graphically and interpret graphs and tables. Finally, scientists often use basic algebra to solve scientific problems and design experiments. For example, the substitution of variables is a common strategy in experiment design. Also, the ability to determine the equation of a curve is valuable in data manipulation, experimentation, and prediction.

Skill 1.3 Analyze the use of biology and other sciences in the design of a technological solution to a given problem.

Science and technology are interdependent as advances in technology often lead to new scientific discoveries and new scientific discoveries often lead to new technologies. Scientists use technology to enhance the study of nature and solve problems that nature presents. Technological design is the identification of a problem and the application of scientific knowledge to solve the problem. While technology and technological design can provide solutions to problems faced by humans, technology must exist within nature and cannot contradict physical or biological principles. In addition, technological solutions are temporary and new technologies typically provide better solutions in the future. Monetary costs, available materials, time, and available tools also limit the scope of technological design and solutions. Finally, technological solutions have intended benefits and unexpected consequences. Scientists must attempt to predict the unintended consequences and minimize any negative impact on nature or society.

The problems and needs, ranging from very simple to highly complex, that technological design can solve are nearly limitless. Disposal of toxic waste, routing of rainwater, crop irrigation, and energy creation are but a few examples of real-world problems that scientists address or attempt to address with technology.

The technological design process has five basic steps:
1. Identify a problem
2. Propose designs and choose between alternative solutions
3. Implement the proposed solution
4. Evaluate the solution and its consequences
5. Report results

After the identification of a problem, the scientist must propose several designs and choose between the alternatives. Scientists often utilize simulations and models in evaluating possible solutions.

Implementation of the chosen solution involves the use of various tools depending on the problem, solution, and technology. Scientists may use both physical tools and objects and computer software.

After implementation of the solution, scientists evaluate the success or failure of the solution against pre-determined criteria. In evaluating the solution, scientists must consider the negative consequences as well as the planned benefits.

Finally, scientists must communicate results in different ways – orally, written, models, diagrams, and demonstrations.

Example:

Problem – toxic waste disposal
Chosen solution – genetically engineered microorganisms to digest waste
Implementation – use genetic engineering technology to create organism capable of converting waste to environmentally safe product
Evaluate – introduce organisms to waste site and measure formation of products and decrease in waste; also evaluate any unintended effects
Report – prepare a written report of results complete with diagrams and figures

Identify a design problem and propose possible solutions, considering such constraints as tools, materials, time, costs, and laws of nature.
In addition to finding viable solutions to design problems, scientists must consider such constraints as tools, materials, time, costs, and laws of nature. Effective implementation of a solution requires adequate tools and materials. Scientists cannot apply scientific knowledge without sufficient technology and appropriate materials (e.g. construction materials, software). Technological design solutions always have costs. Scientists must consider monetary costs, time costs, and the unintended effects of possible solutions. Types of unintended consequences of technological design solutions include adverse environmental impact and safety risks. Finally, technology cannot contradict the laws of nature. Technological design solutions must work within the framework of the natural world.
In evaluating and choosing between potential solutions to a design problem, scientists utilize modeling, simulation, and experimentation techniques. Small-scale modeling and simulation help test the effectiveness and unexpected consequences of proposed solutions while limiting the initial costs. Modeling and simulation may also reveal potential problems that scientists can address prior to full-scale implementation of the solution. Experimentation allows for evaluation of proposed solutions in a controlled environment where scientists can manipulate and test specific variables.

Skill 1.4 Use a variety of software and information technologies (e.g., spreadsheets, graphing utilities, statistical packages, simulations, on-line resources) to model and solve problems in mathematics, science, and technology.

Biologists use a variety of tools and technologies to perform tests, collect and display data, and analyze relationships. Examples of commonly used tools include computer-linked probes, spreadsheets, and graphing calculators.

Biologists use computer-linked probes to measure various environmental factors including temperature, dissolved oxygen, pH, ionic concentration, and pressure. The advantage of computer-linked probes, as compared to more traditional observational tools, is that the probes automatically gather data and present it in an accessible format. This property of computer-linked probes eliminates the need for constant human observation and manipulation.

Biologists use spreadsheets to organize, analyze, and display data. For example, conservation ecologists use spreadsheets to model population growth and development, apply sampling techniques, and create statistical distributions to analyze relationships. Spreadsheet use simplifies data collection and manipulation and allows the presentation of data in a logical and understandable format.

Graphing calculators are another technology with many applications to biology. For example, biologists use algebraic functions to analyze growth, development and other natural processes. Graphing calculators can manipulate algebraic data and create graphs for analysis and observation. In addition, biologists use the matrix function of graphing calculators to model problems in genetics. The use of graphing calculators simplifies the creation of graphical displays including histograms, scatter plots, and line graphs. Biologists can also transfer data and displays to computers for further analysis. Finally, biologists connect computer-linked probes, used to collect data, to graphing calculators to ease the collection, transmission, and analysis of data.

Competency 0002

Understand the historical and contemporary contexts of biological study and the applications of biology and biotechnology to everyday life.

SKILL 2.1 Key events in the history of biological study

Anton van Leeuwenhoek is known as the father of microscopy. In the 1650s, Leeuwenhoek began making tiny lenses which gave magnifications up to 300x. He was the first to see and describe bacteria, yeast plants, and the microscopic life found in water. Over the years, light microscopes have advanced to produce greater clarity and magnification. The scanning electron microscope (SEM) was developed in the 1950s. Instead of light, a beam of electrons passes through the specimen. Scanning electron microscopes have a resolution about one thousand times greater than light microscopes. The disadvantage of the SEM is that the chemical and physical methods used to prepare the sample result in the death of the specimen.

In the late 1800s, Pasteur discovered the role of microorganisms in the cause of disease, pasteurization, and the rabies vaccine. Koch took this observations one step further by formulating that specific diseases were caused by specific pathogens. Koch's postulates are still used as guidelines in the field of microbiology: the same pathogen must be found in every diseased person, the pathogen must be isolated and grown in culture, the disease is induced in experimental animals from the culture, and the same pathogen must be isolated from the experimental animal.

DNA structure was another key event in biological study. In the 1950s, James Watson and Francis Crick discovered the structure of a DNA molecule as that of a double helix. This structure made it possible to explain DNA's ability to replicate and to control the synthesis of proteins.

The use of animals in biological research has expedited many scientific discoveries. Animal research has allowed scientists to learn more about animal biological systems, including the circulatory and reproductive systems. One significant use of animals is for the testing of drugs, vaccines, and other products (such as perfumes and shampoos) before use or consumption by humans. Along with the pros of animal research, the cons are also very significant. The debate about the ethical treatment of animals has been ongoing since the introduction of animals in research. Many people believe the use of animals in research is cruel and unnecessary. Animal use is federally and locally regulated. The purpose of the Institutional Animal Care and Use Committee (IACUC) is to oversee and evaluate all aspects of an institution's animal care and use program.

Skill 2.2 Assess the societal implications of recent developments in biology and biotechnology

Society as a whole impacts biological research. The pressure from the majority of society has led to these bans and restrictions on human cloning research. Human cloning has been restricted in the United States and many other countries. The U.S. legislature has banned the use of federal funds for the development of human cloning techniques. Some individual states have banned human cloning regardless of where the funds originate.

The demand for genetically modified crops by society and industry has steadily increased over the years. Genetic engineering in the agricultural field has led to improved crops for human use and consumption. Crops are genetically modified for increased growth and insect resistance because of the demand for larger and greater quantities of produce.

Wastewater treatment is the process by which contaminants are removed from sewage. In addition to physical and chemical processing, biological methods are used to clean the wastewater and make it suitable for release back into the environment. Indigenous bacteria can be used to remove biological matter dissolved in the water. Activated sludge is the process in which sewage is aerated to allow the growth of various organisms, collectively known as biological floc, including saprophytic bacteria and protozoan. Advances in biotechnology have led to better management of activated sludge, allowing it to removed the bulk of organic material and the conversion of ammonia to nitrogen gas. These advances include moving bed biological reactors, biological aerated filters, and membrane biological reactors.

With advances in biotechnology come those in society who oppose it. Ethical questions come into play when discussing animal and human research. Does it need to be done? What are the effects on humans and animals? There are no right or wrong answers to these questions. There are governmental agencies in place to regulate the use of humans and animals for research.

Science and technology are often referred to as a "double-edged sword". Although advances in medicine have greatly improved the quality and length of life, certain moral and ethical controversies have arisen. Unforeseen environmental problems may result from technological advances. Advances in science have led to an improved economy through biotechnology as applied to agriculture, yet it has put our health care system at risk and has caused the cost of medical care to skyrocket. Society depends on science, yet is necessary that the public be scientifically literate and informed in order to allow potentially unethical procedures to occur. Especially vulnerable are the areas of genetic research and fertility. It is important for science teachers to stay abreast of current research and to involve students in critical thinking and ethics whenever possible.

Competency 0003

Understand the process of scientific inquiry and the role of observation, experimentation, and communication in explaining natural phenomena.

Skill 3.1 Processes by which hypotheses are generated and tested

Science may be defined as a body of knowledge that is systematically derived from study, observations, and experimentation. Its goal is to identify and establish principles and theories that may be applied to solve problems. Pseudoscience, on the other hand, is a belief that is not warranted. There is no scientific methodology or application. Some of the more classic examples of pseudoscience include witchcraft, alien encounters or any topic that is explained by hearsay.

Scientific theory and experimentation must be repeatable. It is also possible to be disproved and is capable of change. Science depends on communication, agreement, and disagreement among scientists. It is composed of theories, laws, and hypotheses.

theory - the formation of principles or relationships which have been verified and accepted.

law - an explanation of events that occur with uniformity under the same conditions (laws of nature, law of gravitation).

hypothesis - an unproved theory or educated guess followed by research to best explain a phenomena. A theory is a proven hypothesis.

Science is limited by the available technology. An example of this would be the relationship of the discovery of the cell and the invention of the microscope. As our technology improves, more hypotheses will become theories and possibly laws. Science is also limited by the data that is able to be collected. Data may be interpreted differently on different occasions. Science limitations cause explanations to be changeable as new technologies emerge.

The first step in scientific inquiry is posing a question to be answered. Next, a hypothesis is formed to provide a plausible explanation. An experiment is then proposed and performed to test this hypothesis. A comparison between the predicted and observed results is the next step. Conclusions are then formed and it is determined whether the hypothesis is correct or incorrect. If incorrect, the next step is to form a new hypothesis and the process is repeated.

Skill 3.2 Analyze ethical issues related to the process of scientific research and reporting.

Scientists are expected to show good conduct in their scientific pursuits.

Conduct here refers to all aspects of scientific activity including experimentation, testing, education, data evaluation, data analysis, data storing, peer review, government funding, the staff, etc.

The following are some of the guiding principles of scientific ethics:

Scientific Honesty: not to fraud, fabricate or misinterpret data for personal gain
Caution: to avoid errors and sloppiness in all scientific experimentation
Credit: give credit where credit is due and not to copy
Responsibility: only to report reliable information to public and not to mislead in the name of science
Freedom: freedom to criticize old ideas, question new research, and freedom to research

Many more principles could be added to this list. Though these principles seem straightforward and clear it is very difficult to put them into practice since they could be interpreted in more ways than one. Nevertheless, it is not an excuse for scientists to overlook these guiding principles of scientific ethics.

To understand scientific ethics, we need to have a clear understanding of ethics. Ethics is defined as a system of public, general rules for guiding human conduct (Gert, 1988). The rules are general in that they are supposed to all people at all times and they are public in that they are not secret codes or practices. Philosophers have given a number of moral theories to justify moral rules, which range from utilitarianism (a theory of ethics that prescribes the quantitative maximization of good consequences for a population. It is a form of consequentialism. This theory was proposed by Mozi, a Chinese philosopher who lived during BC 471-381), Kantianism (a theory proposed by Immanuel Kant, a German philosopher who lived during 1724-1804, which ascribes intrinsic value to rational beings and is the philosophical foundation of contemporary human rights) to social contract theory (a view of the ancient Greeks which states that the person's moral and or political obligations are dependent upon a contract or agreement between them to form society).

The common ethical code described above could be applied to many areas including science. When the general code is applied to a particular area of human life, it then becomes an institutional code. Hence, scientific ethics is an institutional code of conduct that reflects the chief concerns and goals of science. To discuss scientific ethics, we can look at natural phenomena like rain. Rain in the normal sense is extremely useful to us and it is absolutely important that there is water cycle. When rain gets polluted with acid, it becomes acid rain. Here lies the ethical issue of releasing all these pollutants into the atmosphere. Should the scientists communicate the whole truth about acid rain or withhold some information because it may alarm the public. There are many issues like this. Whatever may be the case; scientists are expected to be honest and forthright with the public.

Skill 3.3 Evaluate the appropriateness of a specified experimental design to test a hypothesis.

An experiment is proposed and performed with the sole objective of testing a hypothesis. When evaluating an experiment, it is important to first look at the question it was supposed to answer. How logically did the experiment flow from there? How many variables existed (it is best to only test one variable at a time)? You discover a scientist conducting an experiment with the following characteristics. He has two rows each set up with four stations. The first row has a piece of tile as the base at each station. The second row has a piece of linoleum as the base at each station. The scientist has eight eggs and is prepared to drop one over each station. What is he testing? He is trying to answer whether or not the egg is more likely to break when dropped over one material as opposed to the other. His hypothesis might have been: The egg will be less likely to break when dropped on linoleum. This is a simple experiment. If the experiment was more complicated, or for example, conducted on a microscopic level, one might want to examine the appropriateness of the instruments utilized and their calibration.

Skill 3.4 Analyze the use of models in explaining and investigating natural phenomena.

Once data has been collected and analyzed, it is useful to generalize the information by creating a model. A model is a conceptual representation of a phenomenon. Models are useful in that they clarify relationships, helping us to understand the phenomenon and make predictions about future outcomes. The natural sciences and social sciences employ modeling for this purpose.

Many scientific models are mathematical in nature and contain a set of variables linked by logical and quantitative relationships. These mathematical models may include functions, tables, formulas, graphs, and etc. Typically, such mathematical models include assumptions that restrict them to very specific situations. Often this means they can only provide an *approximate* description of what occurs in the natural world. These assumptions, however, prevent the model from become overly complicated. For a mathematical model to fully explain a natural or social phenomenon, it would have to contain many variables and could become too cumbersome to use. Accordingly, it is critical that assumptions be carefully chosen and thoroughly defined.

Certain models are abstract and simply contain sets of logical principles rather than relying on mathematics. These types of models are generally more vague and are more useful for discovering and understanding new ideas. Abstract models can also include actual physical models built to make concepts more tangible. Abstract models, to an even greater extent than mathematical models, make assumptions and simplify actual phenomena.

Proper scientific models must be able to be tested and verified using experimental data. Often these experimental results are necessary to demonstrate the superiority of a model when two or more conflicting models seek to explain the same phenomenon. Computer simulations are increasingly used in both testing and developing mathematical and even abstract models. These types of simulations are especially useful in situations, such as ecology or manufacturing, where experiments are not feasible or variables are not fully under control.

Competency 0004

Understand principles of measurement and the processes of gathering, organizing, reporting, and interpreting scientific data.

Skill 4.1 Evaluate the appropriateness of a given method or procedure for collecting data for a specified purpose.

Measurements may be taken in different ways. There is an appropriate measuring device for each aspect of biology. A graduated cylinder is used to measure volume. A balance is used to measure mass. A microscope is used to view microscopic objects. A centrifuge is used to separate two or more parts in a liquid sample. The list goes on, but you get the point. For each variable, there is an appropriate way to measure it. The internet and teaching guides are virtually unlimited resources for laboratory ideas. You should be imparting on the students the importance of the method with which they conduct the study, the resource they use to do so, the concept of double checking their work, and the use of appropriate units.

Skill 4.2 Evaluate the appropriateness and limitations of units of measurement, measuring devices, or methods of measurement.

The common instrument used for measuring volume is the graduated cylinder. The unit of measurement is usually in milliliters (mL). It is important for accurate measure to read the liquid in the cylinder at the bottom of the meniscus, the curved surface of the liquid.

The common instrument used is measuring mass is the triple beam balance. The triple beam balance is measured in as low as tenths of a gram and can be estimated to the hundredths of a gram.

The ruler or meter sticks are the most commonly used instruments for measuring length. Measurements in science should always be measured in metric units. Be sure when measuring length that the metric units are used.

Skill 4.3 Knowledge of appropriate and effective graphic representation of data.

The type of graphic representation used to display observations depends on the data that is collected. **Line graphs** are used to compare different sets of related data or to predict data that has not yet be measured. An example of a line graph would be comparing the rate of activity of different enzymes at varying temperatures. A **bar graph** or **histogram** is used to compare different items and make comparisons based on this data. An example of a bar graph would be comparing the ages of children in a classroom. A **pie chart** is useful when organizing data as part of a whole. A good use for a pie chart would be displaying the percent of time students spend on various after school activities.

BIOLOGICAL SCIENCES

Skill 4.4 Analyze relationships between factors (e.g., inverse, direct, linear) as indicated by experimental data.

A direct relationship (also called a positive relationship) is observed when both variables increase (or decrease) at once. The key here is that they both go in the same direction concurrently. An inverse relationship (also called a negative relationship) is present when one variable increases (decreases) while the other variable decreases (increases). In this relationship, the variables are moving in opposing directions.

The individual data points on the graph of a linear relationship cluster around a line of best fit. In other words, a relationship is linear if we can sketch a straight line that roughly fits the data points. Consider the following examples of linear and non-linear relationships.

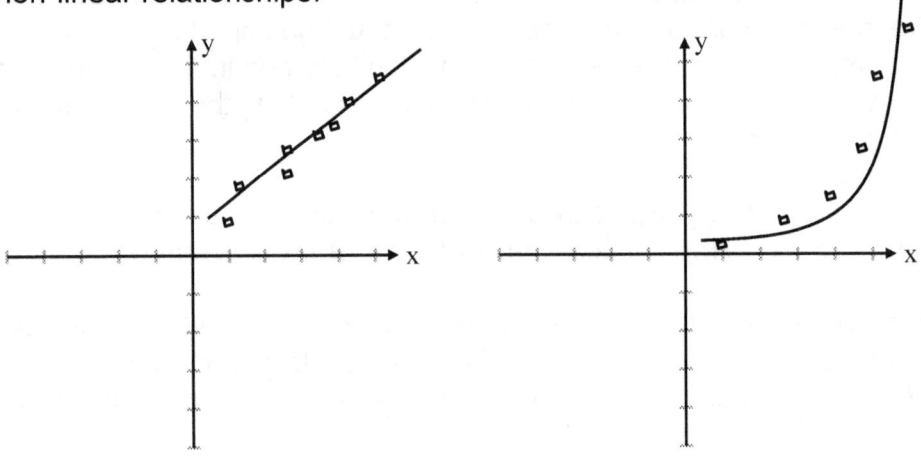

Linear Relationship   Non-Linear Relationship

Note that the non-linear relationship, an exponential relationship in this case, appears linear in parts of the curve. In addition, contrast the preceding graphs to the graph below which is of a data set that shows NO relationship between variables.

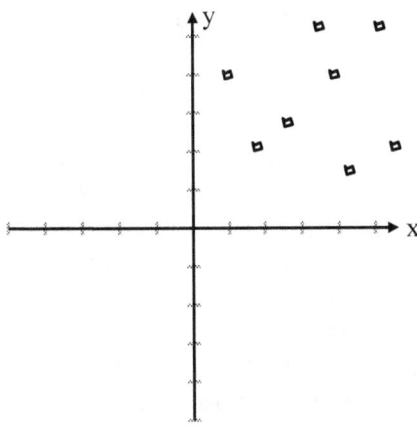

Extrapolation is the process of estimating data points outside a known set of data points. When extrapolating data of a linear relationship, we extend the line of best fit beyond the known values. The extension of the line represents the estimated data points. Extrapolating data is only appropriate if we are relatively certain that the relationship is indeed linear. For example, the death rate of an emerging disease may increase rapidly at first and level off as time goes on. Thus, extrapolating the death rate as if it were linear would yield inappropriately high values at later times. Similarly, extrapolating certain data in a strictly linear fashion, with no restrictions, may yield obviously inappropriate results. For instance, if the number of plant species in a forest were decreasing with time in a linear fashion, extrapolating the data set to infinity would eventually yield a negative number of species, which is clearly unreasonable.

TEACHER CERTIFICATION STUDY GUIDE

Competency 0005

Understand the use of equipment, materials, chemicals, and organisms in biological studies and the application of procedures for their proper, safe, and legal use.

Skill 5.1 Demonstrate knowledge of the appropriate use of laboratory instruments and equipment

Light microscopes are commonly used in high school laboratory experiments. Total magnification is determined by multiplying the ocular (usually 10X) and the objective (usually 10X on low, 40X on high) lenses. Several procedures should be followed to properly care for this equipment.

- Clean all lenses with lens paper only.
- Carry microscopes with two hands; one on the arm and one on the base.
- Always begin focusing on low power, then switch to high power.
- Store microscopes with the low power objective down.
- Always use a coverslip when viewing wet mount slides.
- Bring the objective down to its lowest position then focus moving up to avoid
- breaking the slide or scratching the lens.

Wet mount slides should be made by placing a drop of water on the specimen and then putting a glass coverslip on top of the drop of water. Dropping the coverslip at a forty-five degree angle will help in avoiding air bubbles.

Chromatography uses the principles of capillarity to separate substances such as plant pigments. Molecules of a larger size will move slower up the paper, whereas smaller molecules will move more quickly producing lines of pigment.

An **indicator** is any substance used to assist in the classification of another substance. An example of an indicator is litmus paper. Litmus paper is a way to measure whether a substance is acidic or basic. Blue litmus turns pink when an acid is placed on it and pink litmus turns blue when a base is placed on it. pH paper is a more accurate measure of pH, with the paper turning different colors depending on the pH value.

Spectrophotometry measures percent of light at different wavelengths absorbed and transmitted by a pigment solution.

Centrifugation involves spinning substances at a high speed. The more dense part of a solution will settle to the bottom of the test tube, where the lighter material will stay on top. Centrifugation is used to separate blood into blood cells and plasma, with the heavier blood cells settling to the bottom.

BIOLOGICAL SCIENCES

Electrophoresis uses electrical charges of molecules to separate them according to their size. The molecules, such as DNA or proteins are pulled through a gel towards either the positive end of the gel box (if the material has a negative charge) or the negative end of the gel box (if the material has a positive charge). DNA is negatively charged and moves towards the positive charge.

Glassware

A **beaker** (below left) is a cylindrical cup with a notch at the top. They are often used for making solutions. An **Erlenmeyer** flask (below center) is a conical flask. A liquid in an Erlenmeyer flask will evaporate more slowly than when it is in a beaker and it is easier to swirl about. A **round-bottom flask** (below-right) is also called a Florence flask. It is designed for uniform heating, but it requires a stand to keep it upright.

A **test tube** has a rounded bottom and is designed to hold and to heat small volumes of liquid.

Cleaning glassware becomes more difficult with time, so it should be cleaned soon after the experiment is completed. Wipe off any lubricant with paper towel moistened in a solvent like hexane before washing the glassware. Use a brush with lab soap and water. Acetone may be used to dissolve most organic residues. Spent solvents should be transferred to a waste container for proper disposal.

A **balance** is used to measure mass. To protect the equipment, one should always use a piece of paper between the balance surface and the object being measured. To account for this extra weight, the machine should be tarred (set back to zero) after lying down the paper and before adding the substance.

Skill 5.2 Storing, identifying, and disposing of chemicals and biological materials

All laboratory solutions should be prepared as directed in the lab manual. Care should be taken to avoid contamination. All glassware should be rinsed thoroughly with distilled water before using and cleaned well after use. All solutions should be made with distilled water as tap water contains dissolved particles that may affect the results of an experiment. Unused solutions should be disposed of according to local disposal procedures.

The "Right to Know Law" covers science teachers who work with potentially hazardous chemicals. Briefly, the law states that employees must be informed of potentially toxic chemicals. An inventory must be made available if requested. The inventory must contain information about the hazards and properties of the chemicals. This inventory is to be checked against the "Substance List". Training must be provided on the safe handling and interpretation of the Material Safety Data Sheet.

The following chemicals are potential carcinogens and not allowed in school facilities: Acrylonitriel, Arsenic compounds, Asbestos, Bensidine, Benzene, Cadmium compounds, Chloroform, Chromium compounds, Ethylene oxide, Ortho-toluidine, Nickle powder, and Mercury.

Chemicals should not be stored on bench tops or heat sources. They should be stored in groups based on their reactivity with one another and in protective storage cabinets. All containers within the lab must be labeled. Suspect and known carcinogens must be labeled as such and segregated within trays to contain leaks and spills.

Chemical waste should be disposed of in properly labeled containers. Waste should be separated based on their reactivity with other chemicals.

Biological material should never be stored near food or water used for human consumption. All biological material should be appropriately labeled. All blood and body fluids should be put in a well-contained container with a secure lid to prevent leaking. All biological waste should be disposed of in biological hazardous waste bags.

Material safety data sheets are available for every chemical and biological substance. These are available directly from the company of acquisition or the internet. The manuals for equipment used in the lab should be read and understood before using them.

Skill 5.3 Use of live specimens

No dissections may be performed on living mammalian vertebrates or birds. Lower order life and invertebrates may be used. Biological experiments may be done with all animals except mammalian vertebrates or birds. No physiological harm may result to the animal. All animals housed and cared for in the school must be handled in a safe and humane manner. Animals are not to remain on school premises during extended vacations unless adequate care is provided. Any instructor who intentionally refuses to comply with the laws may be suspended or dismissed.

Pathogenic organisms must never be used for experimentation. Students should adhere to the following rules at all times when working with microorganisms to avoid accidental contamination:

1. Treat all microorganisms as if they were pathogenic.
2. Maintain sterile conditions at all times

Skill 5.4 Dissection and alternatives to dissection

Animals which are not obtained from recognized sources should not be used. Decaying animals or those of unknown origin may harbor pathogens and/or parasites. Specimens should be rinsed before handling. Latex gloves are desirable. If not available, students with sores or scratches should be excused from the activity. Formaldehyde is likely carcinogenic and should be avoided or disposed of according to district regulations. Students objecting to dissections for moral reasons should be given an alternative assignment. Interactive dissections are available online or from software companies for those students who object to performing dissections. There should be no penalty for those students who refuse to physically perform a dissection.

Skill 5.5 Laboratory safety procedures

All science labs should contain the following items of **safety equipment**. Those marked with an asterisk are requirements by state laws.

* fire blanket which is visible and accessible
*Ground Fault Circuit Interrupters (GFCI) within two feet of water supplies
*signs designating room exits
*emergency shower providing a continuous flow of water
*emergency eye wash station which can be activated by the foot or forearm
*eye protection for every student and a means of sanitizing equipment
*emergency exhaust fans providing ventilation to the outside of the building
*master cut-off switches for gas, electric and compressed air. Switches must have permanently attached handles. Cut-off switches must be clearly labeled.
*an ABC fire extinguisher
*storage cabinets for flammable materials
-chemical spill control kit
-fume hood with a motor which is spark proof
-protective laboratory aprons made of flame retardant material
-signs which will alert potential hazardous conditions
-containers for broken glassware, flammables, corrosives, and waste. Containers should be labeled.

Students should wear safety goggles when performing dissections, heating, or while using acids and bases. Hair should always be tied back and objects should never be placed in the mouth. Food should not be consumed while in the laboratory. Hands should always be washed before and after laboratory experiments. In case of an accident, eye washes and showers should be used for eye contamination or a chemical spill that covers the student's body. Small chemical spills should only be contained and cleaned by the teacher. Kitty litter or a chemical spill kit should be used to clean spill. For large spills, the school administration and the local fire department should be notified. Biological spills should also be handled only by the teacher. Contamination with biological waste can be cleaned by using bleach when appropriate.

Accidents and injuries should always be reported to the school administration and local health facilities. The severity of the accident or injury will determine the course of action to pursue.

It is the responsibility of the teacher to provide a safe environment for their students. Proper supervision greatly reduces the risk of injury and a teacher should never leave a class for any reason without providing alternate supervision. After an accident, two factors are considered; **foreseeability** and **negligence**. Foreseeability is the anticipation that an event may occur under certain circumstances. Negligence is the failure to exercise ordinary or reasonable care. Safety procedures should be a part of the science curriculum and a well managed classroom is important to avoid potential lawsuits.

Competency 0006

Understand the functions and interrelatedness of cell structures, and identify the structural features of different types of cells.

Skill 6.1 Compare prokaryotes and eukaryotes

PROKARYOTES

Prokaryotes consist only of bacteria and cyanobacteria (formerly known as blue-green algae). The classification of prokaryotes is in the diagram below.

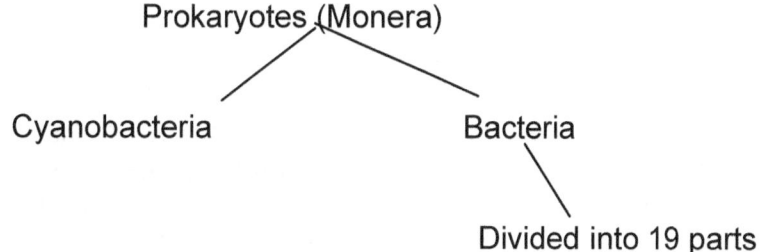

These cells have no defined nucleus or nuclear membrane. The DNA, RNA, and ribosomes float freely within the cell. The cytoplasm has a single chromosome condensed to form a **nucleoid**. Prokaryotes have a thick cell wall made up of amino sugars (glycoproteins). This is for protection, to give the cell shape, and to keep the cell from bursting. It is the **cell wall** of bacteria that is targeted by the antibiotic penicillin. Penicillin works by disrupting the cell wall, thus killing the cell.

The cell wall surrounds the **cell membrane** (plasma membrane). The cell membrane consists of a lipid bilayer that controls the passage of molecules in and out of the cell. Some prokaryotes have a capsule made of polysaccharides that surrounds the cell wall for extra protection from higher organisms.

Many bacterial cells have appendages used for movement called **flagella**. Some cells also have **pili**, which are a protein strand used for attachment of the bacteria. Pili may also be used for sexual conjugation (where the DNA from one bacterial cell is transferred to another bacterial cell).

Prokaryotes are the most numerous and widespread organisms on earth. Bacteria were most likely the first cells and date back in the fossil record to 3.5 billion years ago. Their ability to adapt to the environment allows them to thrive in a wide variety of habitats.

EUKARYOTES

Eukaryotic cells are found in protists, fungi, plants, and animals. Most eukaryotic cells are larger than prokaryotic cells. They contain many organelles, which are membrane bound areas for specific functions. Their cytoplasm contains a cytoskeleton which provides a protein framework for the cell. The cytoplasm also supports the organelles and contains the ions and molecules necessary for cell function. The cytoplasm is contained by the plasma membrane. The plasma membrane allows molecules to pass in and out of the cell. The membrane can bud inward to engulf outside material in a process called endocytosis. Exocytosis is a secretory mechanism, the reverse of endocytosis.

The most significant differentiation between prokaryotes and eukaryotes is that eukaryotes have a **nucleus**. The nucleus is the brain of the cell that contains all of the cell's genetic information. The chromosomes consist of chromatin, which is a complex of DNA and proteins. The chromosomes are tightly coiled to conserve space while providing a large surface area. The nucleus is the site of transcription of the DNA into RNA. The **nucleolus** is where ribosomes are made. There is at least one of these dark-staining bodies inside the nucleus of most eukaryotes. The nuclear envelope is two membranes separated by a narrow space. The envelope contains many pores that let RNA out of the nucleus.

Ribosomes are the site for protein synthesis. Ribosomes may be free floating in the cytoplasm or attached to the endoplasmic reticulum. There may be up to a half a million ribosomes in a cell, depending on how much protein is made by the cell.

The **endoplasmic reticulum** (ER) is folded and provides a large surface area. It is the "roadway" of the cell and allows for transport of materials through and out of the cell. There are two types of ER. Smooth endoplasmic reticulum contains no ribosomes on their surface. This is the site of lipid synthesis. Rough endoplasmic reticulum has ribosomes on their surface. They aid in the synthesis of proteins that are membrane bound or destined for secretion.

Many of the products made in the ER proceed on to the Golgi apparatus. The **Golgi apparatus** functions to sort, modify, and package molecules that are made in the other parts of the cell (like the ER). These molecules are either sent out of the cell or to other organelles within the cell. The Golgi apparatus is a stacked structure to increase the surface area.

Lysosomes are found mainly in animal cells. These contain digestive enzymes that break down food, substances not needed, viruses, damaged cell components and eventually the cell itself. It is believed that lysomomes are responsible for the aging process.

Mitochondria are large organelles that are the site of cellular respiration, where ATP is made to supply energy to the cell. Muscle cells have many mitochondria because they use a great deal of energy. Mitochondria have their own DNA, RNA, and ribosomes and are capable of reproducing by binary fission if there is a greater demand for additional energy. Mitochondria have two membranes: a smooth outer membrane and a folded inner membrane. The folds inside the mitochondria are called cristae. They provide a large surface area for cellular respiration to occur.

Plastids are found only in photosynthetic organisms. They are similar to the mitochondira due to the double membrane structure. They also have their own DNA, RNA, and ribosomes and can reproduce if the need for the increased capture of sunlight becomes necessary. There are several types of plastids. **Chloroplasts** are the sight of photosynthesis. The stroma is the chloroplast's inner membrane space. The stoma encloses sacs called thylakoids that contain the photosynthetic pigment chlorophyll. The chlorophyll traps sunlight inside the thylakoid to generate ATP which is used in the stroma to produce carbohydrates and other products. The **chromoplasts** make and store yellow and orange pigments. They provide color to leaves, flowers, and fruits. The **amyloplasts** store starch and are used as a food reserve. They are abundant in roots like potatoes.

The Endosymbiotic Theory states that mitochondria and chloroplasts were once free living and possibly evolved from prokaryotic cells. At some point in our evolutionary history, they entered the eukaryotic cell and maintained a symbiotic relationship with the cell, with both the cell and organelle benefiting from the relationship. The fact that they both have their own DNA, RNA, ribosomes, and are capable of reproduction helps to confirm this theory.

Found in plant cells only, the **cell wall** is composed of cellulose and fibers. It is thick enough for support and protection, yet porous enough to allow water and dissolved substances to enter. **Vacuoles** are found mostly in plant cells. They hold stored food and pigments. Their large size allows them to fill with water in order to provide turgor pressure. Lack of turgor pressure causes a plant to wilt.

The **cytoskeleton**, found in both animal and plant cells, is composed of protein filaments attached to the plasma membrane and organelles. They provide a framework for the cell and aid in cell movement. They constantly change shape and move about. Three types of fibers make up the cytoskeleton:

1. **Microtubules** – the largest of the three, they make up cilia and flagella for locomotion. Some examples are sperm cells, cilia that line the fallopian tubes and tracheal cilia. Centrioles are also composed of microtubules. They aid in cell division to form the spindle fibers that pull the cell apart into two new cells. Centrioles are not found in the cells of higher plants.

2. **Intermediate filaments** – intermediate in size, they are smaller than microtubules but larger than microfilaments. They help the cell to keep its shape.

3. **Microfilaments** – smallest of the three, they are made of actin and small amounts of myosin (like in muscle tissue). They function in cell movement like cytoplasmic streaming, endocytosis, and ameboid movement. This structure pinches the two cells apart after cell division, forming two new cells.

The following is a diagram of a generalized animal cell.

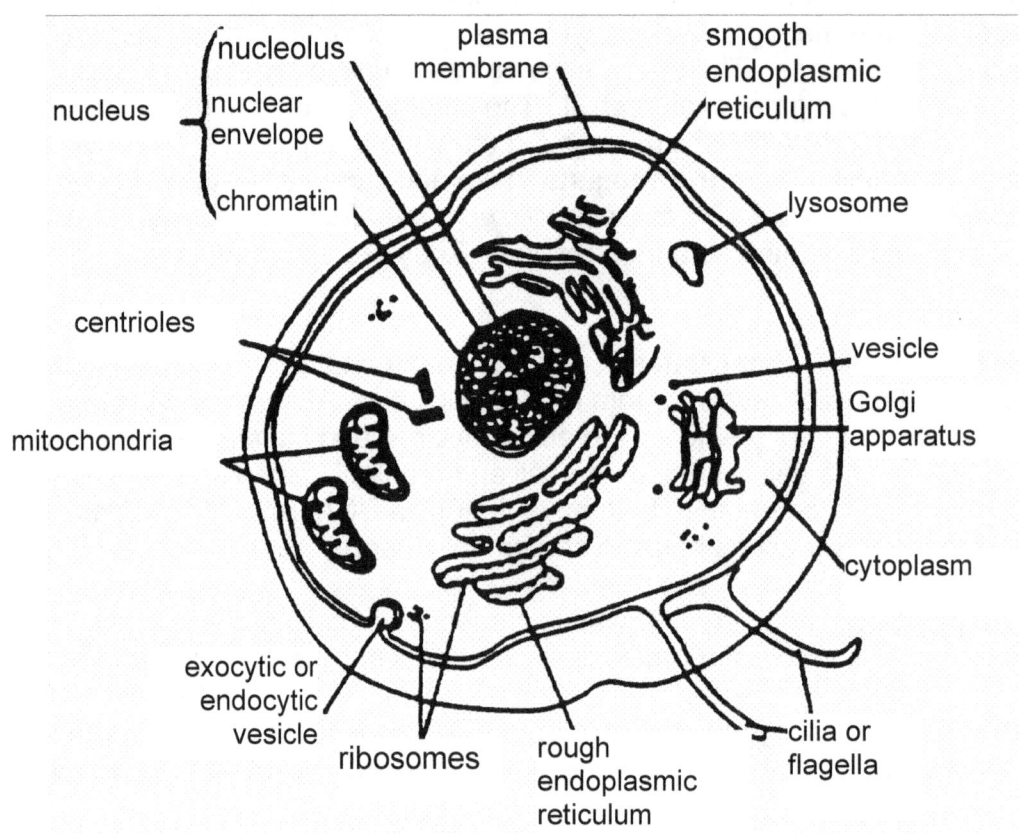

Skill 6.2 Understand the importance of active and passive transport

In order to understand cellular transport, it is important to know about the structure of the cell membrane. All organisms contain cell membranes because they regulate the flow of materials into and out of the cell. The current model for the cell membrane is the Fluid Mosaic Model because of the ability of lipids and proteins to move and change places, giving the membrane fluidity.

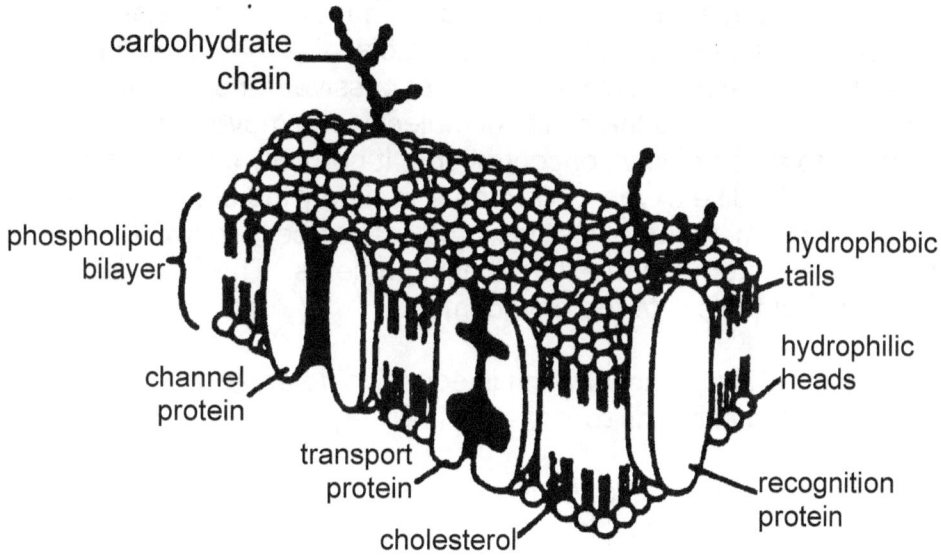

Cell membranes have the following characteristics:

1. They are made of phospholipids which have polar, charged heads with a phosphate group which is hydrophilic (water loving) and two nonpolar lipid tails which are hydrophobic (water fearing). This allows the membrane to orient itself with the polar heads facing the fluid inside and outside the cell and the hydrophobic lipid tails sandwiched in between. Each individual phospholipid is called a micelle.

2. They contain proteins embedded inside (integral proteins) and proteins on the surface (peripheral proteins). These proteins may act as channels for transport, may contain enzymes, may act as receptor sites, may act to stick cells together or may attach to the cytoskeleton to give the cell shape.

3. They contain cholesterol, which alters the fluidity of the membrane.

4. They contain oligosaccharides (small carbohydrate polymers) on the outside of the membrane. These act as markers that help distinguish one cell from another.

5. They contain receptors made of glycoproteins that can attach to certain molecules, like hormones.

Cell transport is necessary to maintain homeostasis, or balance of the cell with its external environment. Cell membranes are selectively permeable, which is the key to transport. Not all molecules may pass through easily. Some molecules require energy or carrier molecules and may only cross when needed.

Passive transport does not require energy and moves the material with the concentration gradient (high to low). Small molecules may pass through the membrane in this manner. Two examples of passive transport include diffusion and osmosis. **Diffusion** is the ability of molecules to move from areas of high concentration to areas of low concentration. It normally involves small uncharged particles like oxygen. **Osmosis** is simply the diffusion of water across a semi-permeable membrane. Osmosis may cause cells to swell or shrink, depending on the internal and external environments. The following terms are used in relation of the cell to the environment.

> **Isotonic** - water concentration is equal inside and outside the cell. Net movement in either direction is basically equal.
>
> **Hypertonic** - "hyper" refers to the amount of dissolved particles. The more particles in a solution, the lower its water concentration. Therefore, when a cell is hypertonic to its environment, there is more water outside the cell than inside. Water will move into the cell and the cell will swell. If the environment is hypertonic to the cell, there is more water inside the cell. Water will move out of the cell and the cell will shrink.
>
> **Hypotonic** - "hypo" again refers to the amount of dissolved particles. The less particles in a solution, the higher its water concentration. When a cell is hypotonic to its environment, there is more water inside the cell than outside. Water will move out of the cell and the cell will shrink. If the environment is hypotonic to the cell, there is more water outside the cell than inside. Water will move into the cell and the cell will swell.

The **facilitated diffusion** mechanism does not require energy, but does require a carrier protein. An example would be insulin, which is needed to carry glucose into the cell.

Active transport requires energy. The energy for this process comes from either ATP or an electrical charge difference. Active transport may move materials either with or against a concentration gradient. Some examples of active transport are:

> -Calcium pumps - actively pump calcium outside of the cell and are important in nerve and muscle transmission.
>
> -Stomach acid pump - exports hydrogen ions to lower the pH of the stomach and increase acidity.
>
> -Sodium-Potassium pump - maintains an electrical difference across the cell. This is useful in restoring ion balance so nerves can continue to function. It exchanges sodium ions for potassium ions across the plasma membrane in animal cells.

Active transport involves a membrane potential which is a charge on the membrane. The charge works like a magnet and may cause transport proteins to alter their shape, thus allowing substances in or out of the cell.

The transport of large molecules depends on the fluidity of the membrane which is controlled by cholesterol in the membrane. **Exocytosis** is the release of large particles by the vesicles fusing with the plasma membrane. In the process of **endocytosis**, the cell takes in macromolecules and particulate matter by forming vesicles derived from the plasma membrane. There are three types of endocytosis in animal cells. **Phagocytosis** is when a particle is engulfed by pseudopodia and packaged in a vacuole. In **pinocytosis**, the cell takes in extracellular fluid in small vesicles. **Receptor-mediated endocytosis** is when the membrane vesicles bud inward to allow a cell to take in large amounts of certain substances. The vesicles have proteins with receptors that are specific for the substance.

Competency 0007

Understand basic chemistry and biochemistry, and use this understanding to analyze the role of biologically important elements and compounds in living organisms.

Skill 7.1 Compare and contrast hydrogen, ionic, and covalent bonds

Chemical bonds are formed when atoms with incomplete valence shells share or completely transfer their valence electrons. There are three types of chemical bonds, covalent and ionic bonds being stronger than hydrogen bonds.

Covalent bonding is the sharing of a pair of valence electrons by two atoms. A simple example of this is two hydrogen atoms. Each hydrogen atom has one valence electron in its outer shell, therefore the two hydrogen atoms come together to share their electrons. Some atoms share two pairs of valence electrons, like two oxygen atoms. This is called a double covalent bond.

The attraction for the electrons of a covalent bond is called electronegativity. The stronger the electronegativity of an atom, the more it pulls the shared electrons towards itself. Electronegativity defines whether atoms are in a polar or nonpolar covalent bond. In **nonpolar covalent bonds**, the electrons are shared equally, thus the electronegativity of the two atoms is the same. This type of bonding usually occurs between two of the same atoms. A **polar covalent bond** is mostly formed when different atoms join, as in hydrogen and oxygen to create water. In this case, oxygen is more electronegative than hydrogen so the oxygen pulls the hydrogen electrons toward itself.

Ionic bonds are formed when one electron is stripped away from its atom to join another atom. In example of this is sodium chloride (NaCl). A single electron on the outer shell of sodium joins the chloride atom with seven electrons in its outer shell. The sodium now has a +1 charge and the chloride now has a -1 charge. The charges attract each other to form an ionic bond. Ionic compounds are called salts. In a dry salt crystal, the bond is so strong it requires a great deal of strength to break it apart. But, place the salt crystal in water, and the bond dissolves easily as the attraction between the two atoms decreases.

The weakest of the three bonds is the **hydrogen bond**. A hydrogen bond is formed when one electronegative atom shares a hydrogen atom with another electronegative atom. An example of a hydrogen bond is water (H_2O) bonding with ammonia (NH_3). The H^+ attracts the negatively charged nitrogen in a weak bond. Weak hydrogen bonds are beneficial because they can briefly form, the atoms can respond to one another, and then break apart to bond to another. This is a very important role in the chemistry of life.

Skill 7.2 Analyze the structure and function of carbohydrates, lipids, proteins, and nucleic acids

A compound consists of two or more elements. There are four major chemical compounds found in the cells and bodies of living things. These include carbohydrates, lipids, proteins and nucleic acids.

Monomers are the simplest unit of structure. **Monomers** can be combined to form **polymers**, or long chains, making a large variety of molecules possible. Monomers combine through the process of condensation reaction (also called dehydration synthesis). In this process, one molecule of water is removed between each of the adjoining molecules. In order to break the molecules apart in a polymer, water molecules are added between monomers, thus breaking the bonds between them. This is called **hydrolysis**.

Carbohydrates contain a ratio of two hydrogen atoms for each carbon and oxygen $(CH_2O)_n$. Carbohydrates include sugars and starches. They function in the release of energy. **Monosaccharides** are the simplest sugars and include glucose, fructose, and galactose. They are major nutrients for cells. In cellular respiration, the cells extract the energy in glucose molecules. **Disaccharides** are made by joining two monosaccharides by condensation to form a glycosidic linkage (covalent bond between two monosaccharides). Maltose is formed from the combination of two glucose molecules, lactose is formed from joining glucose and galactose, and sucrose is formed from the combination of glucose and fructose. **Polysaccharides** consist of many monomers joined. They are storage material hydrolyzed (EXPLAIN HYDROLYSIS) as needed to provide sugar for cells or building material for structures protecting the cell. Examples of polysaccharides include starch, glycogen, cellulose and chitin.

> **Starch** - major energy storage molecule in plants. It is a polymer consisting of glucose monomers.
> **Glycogen** - major energy storage molecule in animals. It is made up of many glucose molecules.
> **Cellulose** - found in plant cell walls, its function is structural. Many animals lack the enzymes necessary to hydrolyze cellulose, so it simply adds bulk (fiber) to the diet.
> **Chitin** - found in the exoskeleton of arthropods and fungi. Chitin contains an amino sugar (glycoprotein).

Lipids are composed of glycerol (an alcohol) and three fatty acids. Lipids are **hydrophobic** (water fearing) and will not mix with water. There are three important families of lipids, fats, phospholipids and steroids.

Fats consist of glycerol (alcohol) and three fatty acids. Fatty acids are long carbon skeletons. The nonpolar carbon-hydrogen bonds in the tails of fatty acids are why they are hydrophobic. Fats are solids at room temperature and come from animal sources (butter, lard).

Phospholipids are a vital component in cell membranes. In a phospholipid, one or two fatty acids are replaced by a phosphate group linked to a nitrogen group. They consist of a **polar** (charged) head that is hydrophilic or water loving and a **nonpolar** (uncharged) tail which is hydrophobic or water fearing. This allows the membrane to orient itself with the polar heads facing the interstitial fluid found outside the cell and the internal fluid of the cell.

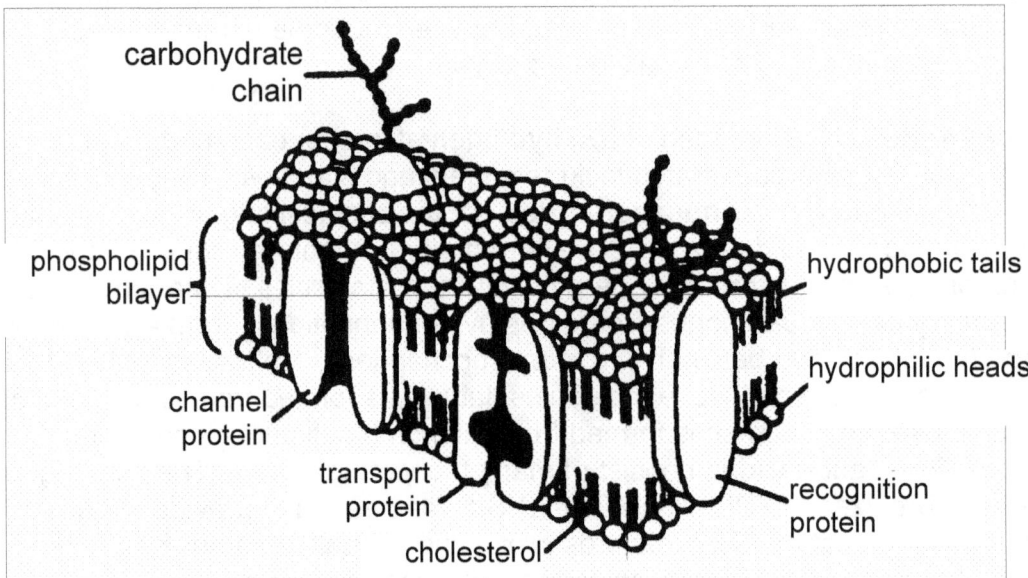

Steroids are insoluble and are composed of a carbon skeleton consisting of four inter-connected rings. An important steroid is cholesterol, which is the precursor from which other steroids are synthesized. Hormones, including cortisone, testosterone, estrogen, and progesterone, are steroids. Their insolubility keeps them from dissolving in body fluids.

Proteins compose about fifty percent of the dry weight of animals and bacteria. Proteins function in structure and aid in support (connective tissue, hair, feathers, quills), storage of amino acids (albumin in eggs, casein in milk), transport of substances (hemoglobin), hormonal to coordinate body activities (insulin), membrane receptor proteins, contraction (muscles, cilia, flagella), body defense (antibodies), and as enzymes to speed up chemical reactions. All proteins are made of twenty **amino acids**. An amino acid contains an amino group and an acid group. The radical group varies and defines the amino acid. Amino acids form through condensation reactions with the removal of water. The bond that is formed between two amino acids is called a peptide bond. Polymers of amino acids are called polypeptide chains. An analogy can be drawn between the twenty amino acids and the alphabet.

Millions of words can be formed using an alphabet of only twenty-six letters. This diversity is also possible using only twenty amino acids. This results in the formation of many different proteins, whose structure defines the function.

There are four levels of protein structure: primary, secondary, tertiary, and quaternary.

Primary structure is the protein's unique sequence of amino acids. A slight change in primary structure can affect a protein's conformation and its ability to function. **Secondary structure** is the coils and folds of polypeptide chains. The coils and folds are the result of hydrogen bonds along the polypeptide backbone. The secondary structure is either in the form of an alpha helix or a pleated sheet. The alpha helix is a coil held together by hydrogen bonds. A pleated sheet is the polypeptide chain folding back and forth. The hydrogen bonds between parallel regions hold it together. **Tertiary structure** is formed by bonding between the side chains of the amino acids. Disulfide bridges are created when two sulfhydryl groups on the amino acids bond together to form a strong covalent bond. **Quaternary structure** is the overall structure of the protein from the aggregation of two or more polypeptide chains. An example of this is hemoglobin. Hemoglobin consists of two kinds of polypeptide chains.

Nucleic acids consist of DNA (deoxyribonucleic acid) and RNA (ribonucleic acid). Nucleic acids contain the instructions for the amino acid sequence of proteins and the instructions for replicating. The monomer of nucleic acids is called a nucleotide. A nucleotide consists of a 5 carbon sugar, (deoxyribose in DNA, ribose in RNA), a phosphate group, and a nitrogenous base. The base sequence codes for the instructions. There are five bases: adenine, thymine, cytosine, guanine, and uracil. Uracil is found only in RNA and replaces the thymine. A summary of nucleic acid structure can be seen in the table below:

	SUGAR	PHOSPHATE	BASES
DNA	deoxyribose	present	adenine, thymine, cytosine, guanine
RNA	ribose	present	adenine, uracil, cytosine, guanine

Due to the molecular structure, adenine will always pair with thymine in DNA or uracil in RNA. Cytosine always pairs with guanine in both DNA and RNA. This allows for the symmetry of the DNA molecule seen in the next page.

Adenine and thymine (or uracil) are linked by two covalent bonds and cytosine and guanine are linked by three covalent bonds. The guanine and cytosine bonds are harder to break apart than thymine (uracil) and adenine because of the greater number of these bonds. The DNA molecule is called a double helix due to its twisted ladder shape.

Skill 7.3 Analyze the properties of water and its significance to living organisms

Water is necessary for life. Its properties are due to its molecular structure and it is an important solvent in biological compounds. Water is a polar substance. This means it is formed by covalent bonds that make it electrically lopsided.

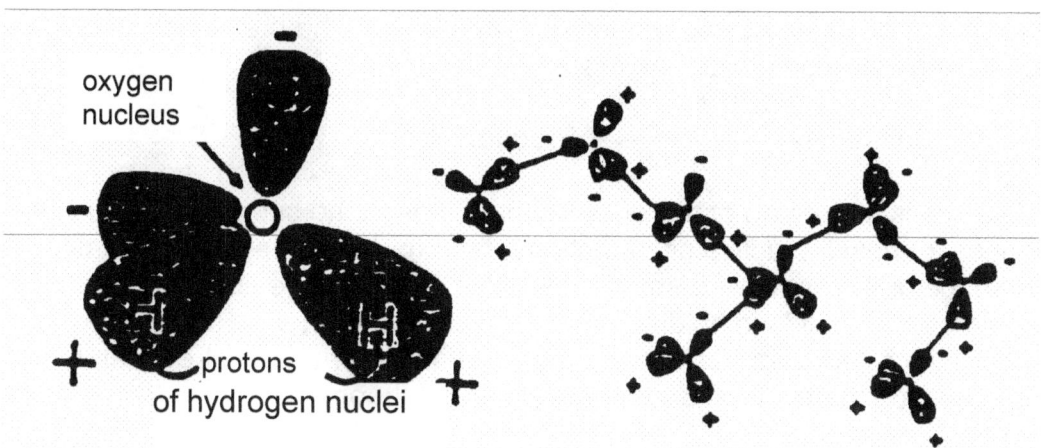

A water molecule showing polarity created by covalent bonds.

Hydrogen bonding between water molecules.

Water molecules are attracted to other water molecules due to this electrical attraction and allows for two important properties: **adhesion** and **cohesion**.

Adhesion is when water sticks to other substances like the xylem of a stem which aids the water in traveling up the stem to the leaves.

Cohesion is the ability of water molecules to stick to each other by hydrogen bonds. This allows for surface tension on a body of water or capillarity which allows water to move through vessels. Surface tension is how difficult it is to stretch or break the surface of a liquid. Cohesion allows water to move against gravity.

There are several other important properties of water. Water is a good solvent. An aqueous solution is one in which water is the solvent. It provides a medium for chemical reactions to occur. Water has a high specific heat of 1 calorie per gram per degree Celsius, allowing it to cool and warm slowly, allowing organisms to adapt to temperature changes. Water has a high boiling point it is a good coolant. Its ability to evaporate stabilizes the environment and allows organisms to maintain body temperature. Water has a high freezing point and a lower density as a solid than as a liquid. Water is most dense at four degrees centigrade. This allows ice to   float on top of water so a whole body of water does not freeze during the winter. In this way, animals may survive the winter.

Skill 7.4 Analyze the structure and function of enzymes and factors

Enzymes act as biological catalysts to speed up reactions. Enzymes are the most diverse of all types of proteins. They are not used up in a reaction and are recyclable. Each enzyme is specific for a single reaction. Enzymes act on a substrate. The substrate is the material to be broken down or put back together.

Most enzymes end in the suffix -ase (lipase, amylase). The prefix is the substrate being acted on (lipids, sugars).

$$\text{Substrate} \xrightarrow{\text{Enzyme}} \text{Product}$$

The active site is the region of the enzyme that binds to the substrate. There are two theories for how the active site functions. The **lock and key theory** states that the shape of the enzyme is specific because it fits into the substrate like a key fits into a lock. It aids in holding molecules close together so reactions can easily occur. The **Induced fit theory** states that an enzyme can stretch and bend to fit the substrate. This is the most accepted theory.

Many factors can affect enzyme activity. Temperature and pH are two of those factors. The temperature can affect the rate of reaction of an enzyme. The optimal pH for enzymes is between 6 and 8, with a few enzymes whose optimal pH falls out of this range.

Cofactors aid in the enzyme's function. Cofactors may be inorganic or organic. Organic cofactors are known as coenzymes. An example of a coenzyme is vitamins. Some chemicals can inhibit an enzymes function. **Competitive inhibitors** block the substrate from entering the active site of the enzyme to reduce productivity. **Noncompetitive inhibitors** bind to the enzyme in a location not in the active site but still interrupt substrate binding. In most cases, noncompetitive inhibitors alter the shape of the enzyme. An **allosteric enzyme** can exist in two shapes; they are active in one form and inactive in the other. Overactive enzymes may cause metabolic diseases.

Competency 0008

Understand the processes of photosynthesis and cellular respiration and their relationships to cell structure and function.

Skill 8.1 Analyze limiting factors that affect the yield of energy from the breakdown of organic molecules in a cell.

Several environmental and cellular factors affect the rate of photosynthesis and cellular respiration. The three main environmental factors affecting photosynthesis are light intensity, carbon dioxide concentration, and temperature. In addition, cellular and physical plant characteristics including leaf shape, nitrogen content, and molecular carrier (e.g. NADP, FAD) concentration affect photosynthetic rates. The main factors affecting cellular respiration rates are temperature, oxygen concentration, and molecular carrier concentration.

The environmental factors light intensity, carbon dioxide concentration, and temperature greatly affect photosynthesis. First, rates of photosynthesis increase as light intensity increases to a certain plateau level. Too much light can inactivate a plant's photosynthetic system. In addition, the rate of photosynthesis increases as carbon dioxide increases until other factors become limiting. Finally, the rate of photosynthesis increases as temperature increases until the temperature reaches a critical point that begins to damage the plant.

The physical and cellular factors affecting photosynthesis are leaf shape, molecular carrier concentration, and nitrogen content. The shape of a leaf affects the efficiency of light absorption. The concentration of molecular carrier molecules such as NADP and FAD affects the rate and efficiency of electron transport. Finally, nitrogen is a necessary nutrient for proper plant functioning.

The main factors affecting cellular respiration rates are temperature, oxygen content, and molecular carrier concentration. Cellular processes, including respiration, generally increase as temperature increases to a certain plateau level. In addition, oxygen content affects the rate, type (anaerobic versus aerobic), and ultimate energy yield of respiration. Aerobic respiration, requiring oxygen, yields more energy than anaerobic respiration that proceeds in the absence of adequate levels of oxygen. Finally, as with photosynthesis, the cellular concentration of NADP and FAD affects the rate and efficiency of respiration.

Skill 8.2 Understand the significance of photosynthesis and respiration to living organisms

Cellular respiration is the metabolic pathway in which food (glucose, etc.) is broken down to produce energy in the form of ATP. Both plants and animals utilize respiration to create energy for metabolism. In respiration, energy is released by the transfer of electrons in a process know as an **oxidation-reduction (redox)** reaction. The oxidation phase of this reaction is the loss of an electron and the reduction phase is the gain of an electron. Redox reactions are important for the stages of respiration.

Glycolysis is the first step in respiration. It occurs in the cytoplasm of the cell and does not require oxygen. Each of the ten stages of glycolysis is catalyzed by a specific enzyme. The following is a summary of those stages.

In the first stage the reactant is glucose. For energy to be released from glucose, it must be converted to a reactive compound. This conversion occurs through the phosphorylation of a molecule of glucose by the use of two molecules of ATP. This is an investment of energy by the cell. The six carbon product, called fructose -1,6- bisphosphate, breaks into two 3-carbon molecules of sugar. A phosphate group is added to each sugar molecule and hydrogen atoms are removed. Hydrogen is picked up by NAD^+ (a vitamin). Since there are two sugar molecules, two molecules of NADH are formed. The reduction (adding of hydrogen) of NAD allows the potential of energy transfer. As the phosphate bonds are broken, ATP is made. Two ATP molecules are generated as each original 3 carbon sugar molecule is converted to pyruvic acid (pyruvate). A total of four ATP molecules are made in the four stages. Since two molecules of ATP were needed to start the reaction in stage 1, there is a net gain of two ATP molecules at the end of glycolysis. This accounts for only two percent of the total energy in a molecule of glucose.

Beginning with pyruvate, which was the end product of glycolysis, the following steps occur before entering the **Krebs cycle**.

1. Pyruvic acid is changed to acetyl-CoA (coenzyme A). This is a three carbon pyruvic acid molecule which has lost one molecule of carbon dioxide (CO_2) to become a two carbon acetyl group. Pyruvic acid loses a hydrogen to NAD^+ which is reduced to NADH.

2. Acetyl CoA enters the Krebs cycle. For each molecule of glucose it started with, two molecules of Acetyl CoA enter the Krebs cycle (one for each molecule of pyruvic acid formed in glycolysis).

The **Krebs cycle** (also known as the citric acid cycle), occurs in four major steps. First, the two-carbon acetyl CoA combines with a four-carbon molecule to form a six-carbon molecule of citric acid. Next, two carbons are lost as carbon dioxide (CO_2) and a four-carbon molecule is formed to become available to join with CoA to form citric acid again. Since we started with two molecules of CoA, two turns of the Krebs cycle are necessary to process the original molecule of glucose. In the third step, eight hydrogen atoms are released and picked up by FAD and NAD (vitamins and electron carriers).
Lastly, for each molecule of CoA (remember there were two to start with) you get:

> 3 molecules of NADH x 2 cycles
> 1 molecule of $FADH_2$ x 2 cycles
> 1 molecule of ATP x 2 cycles

Therefore, this completes the breakdown of glucose. At this point, a total of four molecules of ATP have been made; two from glycolysis and one from each of the two turns of the Krebs cycle. Six molecules of carbon dioxide have been released; two prior to entering the Krebs cycle, and two for each of the two turns of the Krebs cycle. Twelve carrier molecules have been made; ten NADH and two $FADH_2$. These carrier molecules will carry electrons to the electron transport chain. ATP is made by substrate level phosphorylation in the Krebs cycle. Notice that the Krebs cycle in itself does not produce much ATP, but functions mostly in the transfer of electrons to be used in the electron transport chain where the most ATP is made.

In the **Electron Transport Chain,** NADH transfers electrons from glycolysis and the Kreb's cycle to the first molecule in the chain of molecules embedded in the inner membrane of the mitochondrion. Most of the molecules in the electron transport chain are proteins. Nonprotein molecules are also part of the chain and are essential for the catalytic functions of certain enzymes. The electron transport chain does not make ATP directly. Instead, it breaks up a large free energy drop into a more manageable amount. The chain uses electrons to pump H^+ across the mitochondrion membrane. The H^+ gradient is used to form ATP synthesis in a process called **chemiosmosis** (oxidative phosphorylation). ATP synthetase and energy generated by the movement of hydrogen ions coming off of NADH and $FADH_2$ builds ATP from ADP on the inner membrane of the mitochondria. Each NADH yields three molecules of ATP (10 x 3) and each $FADH_2$ yields two molecules of ATP (2 x 2). Thus, the electron transport chain and oxidative phosphorylation produces 34 ATP.

So, the net gain from the whole process of respiration is 36 molecules of ATP:
  Glycolysis - 4 ATP made, 2 ATP spent = net gain of 2 ATP
  Acetyl CoA- 2 ATP used
  Krebs cycle - 1 ATP made for each turn of the cycle = net gain of 2 ATP
  Electron transport chain - 34 ATP gained

Photosynthesis is an anabolic process that stores energy in the form of a three carbon sugar. We will use glucose as an example for this section. Photosynthesis is done only by organisms that contain chloroplasts (plants, some bacteria, some protists). There are a few terms to be familiar with when discussing photosynthesis.

An **autotroph** (self feeder) is an organism that make its own food from the energy of the sun or other elements. Autotrophs include:

1. **photoautotrophs** - make food from light and carbon dioxide releasing
oxygen that can be used for respiration.
2. **chemoautotrophs** - oxidize sulfur and ammonia; this is done by some
bacteria.

Heterotrophs (other feeder) are organisms that must eat other living things for their energy. **Consumers** are the same as heterotroph; all animals are heterotrophs. **Decomposers** break down once living things. Bacteria and fungi are examples of decomposers. **Scavengers** eat dead things. Examples of scavengers are bacteria, fungi and some animals.

The **chloroplast** is the site of photosynthesis. It is similar to the mitochondria due to the increased surface area of the thylakoid membrane. It also contains a fluid called stroma between the stacks of thylakoids. The thylakoid membrane contains pigments (chlorophyll) that are capable of capturing light energy.

Photosynthesis reverses the electron flow. Water is split by the chloroplast into hydrogen and oxygen. The oxygen is given off as a waste product as carbon dioxide is reduced to sugar (glucose). This requires the input of energy, which comes from the sun.

Photosynthesis occurs in two stages: the light reactions and the Calvin cycle (dark reactions). The conversion of solar energy to chemical energy occurs in the light reactions. Electrons are transferred by the absorption of light by chlorophyll and cause the water to split, releasing oxygen as a waste product. The chemical energy that is created in the light reaction is in the form of NADPH. ATP is also produced by a process called photophosphorylation. These forms of energy are produced in the thylakoids and are used in the Calvin cycle to produce sugar.

The second stage of photosynthesis is the **Calvin cycle**. Carbon dioxide in the air is incorporated into organic molecules already in the chloroplast. The NADPH produced in the light reaction is used as reducing power for the reduction of the carbon to carbohydrate. ATP from the light reaction is also needed to convert carbon dioxide to carbohydrate (sugar).

The process of photosynthesis is made possible by the presence of the sun. Visible light ranges in wavelengths of 750 nanometers (red light) to 380 nanometers (violet light). As wavelength decreases, the amount of energy available increases. Light is carried as photons, which is a fixed quantity of energy. Light is reflected (what we see), transmitted, or absorbed (what the plant uses). The plant's pigments capture light of specific wavelengths. Remember that the light that is reflected is what we see as color. Plant pigments include:

Chlorophyll *a* - reflects green/blue light; absorbs red light
Chlorophyll *b* - reflects yellow/green light; absorbs red light
Carotenoids - reflects yellow/orange; absorbs violet/blue

The pigments absorb photons. The energy from the light excites electrons in the chlorophyll that jump to orbitals with more potential energy and reach an "excited" or unstable state.

The formula for photosynthesis is:

$$CO_2 + H_2O + \text{energy (from sunlight)} \rightarrow C_6H_{12}O_6 + O_2$$

The high energy electrons are trapped by primary electron acceptors which are located on the thylakoid membrane. These electron acceptors and the pigments form reaction centers called photosystems that are capable of capturing light energy. Photosystems contain a reaction-center chlorophyll that releases an electron to the primary electron acceptor. This transfer is the first step of the light reactions. There are two photosystems, named according to their date of discovery, not their order of occurrence.

Photosystem I is composed of a pair of chlorophyll *a* molecules. Photosystem I is also called P700 because it absorbs light of 700 nanometers. Photosystem I makes ATP whose energy is needed to build glucose.

Photosystem II - this is also called P680 because it absorbs light of 680 nanometers. Photosystem II produces ATP + $NADPH_2$ and the waste gas oxygen.

Both photosystems are bound to the **thylakoid membrane**, close to the electron acceptors.

The production of ATP is termed **photophosphorylation** due to the use of light. Photosystem I uses cyclic photophosphorylation because the pathway occurs in a cycle. It can also use noncyclic photophosphorylation which starts with light and ends with glucose. Photosystem II uses noncyclic photophosphorylation only.

BIOLOGICAL SCIENCES

Below is a diagram of the relationship between cellular respiration and photosynthesis.

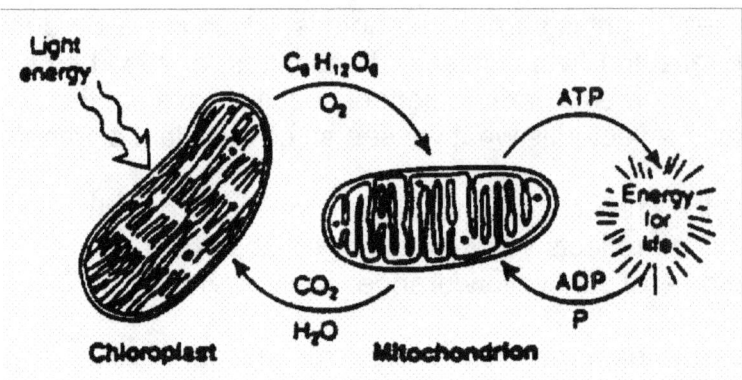

Skill 8.3 Evaluate the significance of chloroplast structure and mitochondrion structure in the processes of photosynthesis and respiration.

Within chloroplasts, the process of photosynthesis takes place across a membrane to convert light energy into chemical energy stored in sugar. In mitochondria, a similar reaction, cellular respiration, also takes place across a membrane to create ATP. The processes are complementary in that photosynthesis allows energy from light to enter the food chain (as sugar) and cellular respiration harnesses that energy (from sugar) into a form usable by all other processes essential to maintaining life (ATP). These two reactions are among the most important in the carbon cycle, the series of biochemical reactions that move carbon from the atmosphere, to living things, into geological structures, and back to the atmosphere.

Chloroplasts and mitochondria are similar in their suspected origins. Most biologists now believe that both these organelles were originally separate prokaryotic organisms that were drawn into cells as endosymbionts (organisms that live inside other organisms for their mutual benefit). This hypothesized origin of these organelles is referred to as the endosymbiotic theory. This may explain the similar structures of chloroplasts and mitochondria; both have inner and outer membranes. The outer membrane may correspond to the cell membrane of the original endosymbiont. Additionally, both mitochondria and chloroplasts have their own DNA and it exists in circular form, as it does in prokaryotes. Both these organelles are also able to synthesize proteins using ribosomes similar to those seen in bacteria. Finally, both mitochondria and chloroplasts are able to reproduce themselves independently of the cell as a whole. At present, it is suspected that mitochondria evolved from aerobic bacteria and chloroplasts from cyanobacteria.

There are also similarities in the manner in which these organelles accomplish their unique energy transformation. Both mitochondria and chloroplasts have highly specific trans-membranous proteins that actually perform the energy transformation. In mitochondria, the inner membrane is the location of all the integral proteins needed in the electron tansport chain and ATP synthase. The maintenance of a proton gradient across the inner membrane is key to the process of ATP synthesis. Chloroplasts have one more membrane bound compartment than mitochondria: the thylakoids. The thylakoid membrane contains the proteins of the electron transport change and the chlorophyll-containing photosystems that are excited by light. The proton gradient is established across this membrane, rather than across the inner membrane, as happens in cellular respiration. However, photosynthesis, just like cellular respiration, relies on cross-membrane fluxes to drive biosynthesis.

Skill 8.4 Compare C3 and C4 photosynthesis.

While photosynthesis is common to all plant species, the specific mechanism often differs. Two major types of photosynthesis are C3 and C4. C3 photosynthesis is the typical mechanism of photosynthesis that most plants use. C4 photosynthesis, on the other hand, is an adaptation to arid environmental conditions because it results in more efficient use of water. C3 and C4 photosynthesis differ in several key ways.

In C3 photosynthesis, the first carbon compound formed from carbon dioxide contains three carbon atoms. C3 plants use a single enzyme, ribulosodiphosphatcarboxylase (RUBISCO), to collect carbon dioxide from the air and carry out photosynthesis. Finally, C3 photosynthesis takes place in cells throughout the leaf.

In C4 photosynthesis, the first carbon compound formed from carbon dioxide contains four carbon atoms. In contrast to C3 plants, C4 plants use two enzymes for photosynthesis. One enzyme, phosphoenolpyruvatcarboxylase (PEP Carboxylase), collects carbon dioxide and delivers it directly to the second enzyme, RUBISCO. This adaptation increases the rate of photosynthesis in high light intensity and high temperature conditions. In addition, unlike in C3 plants, C4 photosynthesis only occurs in internal leaf cells. Thus, the C4 adaptations allow for more efficient photosynthesis in dry conditions and minimize loss of water. The faster and more efficient uptake and delivery of carbon dioxide allows the plant to keep its stomata closed longer, limiting water loss, while still acquiring adequate amounts of carbon dioxide.

Competency 0009

Understand the structure and function of DNA and RNA.

Skill 9.1 DNA replication, potential errors, and implications of these errors

DNA replicates semiconservatively. This means the two original strands are conserved and serve as a template for the new strand.

In DNA replication, the first step is to separate the two strands. As they separate, they need to unwind the supercoils to reduce tension. An enzyme called **helicase** unwinds the DNA as the replication fork proceeds and **topoisomerases** relieve the tension by nicking one strand and letting the supercoil relax. Once the strands have been separated, they need to be stabilized. Single stranded binding proteins (SSBs) bind to the single strands until the DNA is replicated.

An RNA polymerase called primase adds ribonucleotides to the DNA template to initiate DNA synthesis. This short RNA-DNA hybrid is called a **primer**. Once the DNA is single stranded, **DNA polymerases** add nucleotides in the 5' → 3' direction.

As DNA synthesis proceeds along the replication fork, it becomes obvious that replication is semi-discontinuous; meaning one strand is synthesized in the direction the replication fork is moving and the other is synthesizing in the opposite direction. The strand that is continuously synthesized is the **leading strand** and the discontinuously synthesized strand is the **lagging strand**. As the replication fork proceeds, new primer is added to the lagging strand and it is synthesized discontinuously in fragments called **Okazaki fragments**.

The RNA primers that remain need to be removed and replaced with deoxyribonucleotides. DNA polymerase has 5' → 3' polymerase activity and has 3' → 5' exonuclease activity. This enzyme binds to the nick between the Okazaki fragment and the RNA primer. It removes the primer and adds deoxyribonucleotides in the 5' → 3' direction. The nick still remains until **DNA ligase** seals it with the final product being a double stranded segment of DNA.

Once the double stranded segment is replicated, there is a proofreading system by DNA replication enzymes. In eukaryotes, DNA polymerases have 3' → 5' exonuclease activity—they move backwards and remove nucleotides where the enzyme recognizes an error, then it adds the correct nucleotide in the 5' → 3' direction. In E. coli, DNA polymerase II synthesizes DNA during repair of DNA damage.

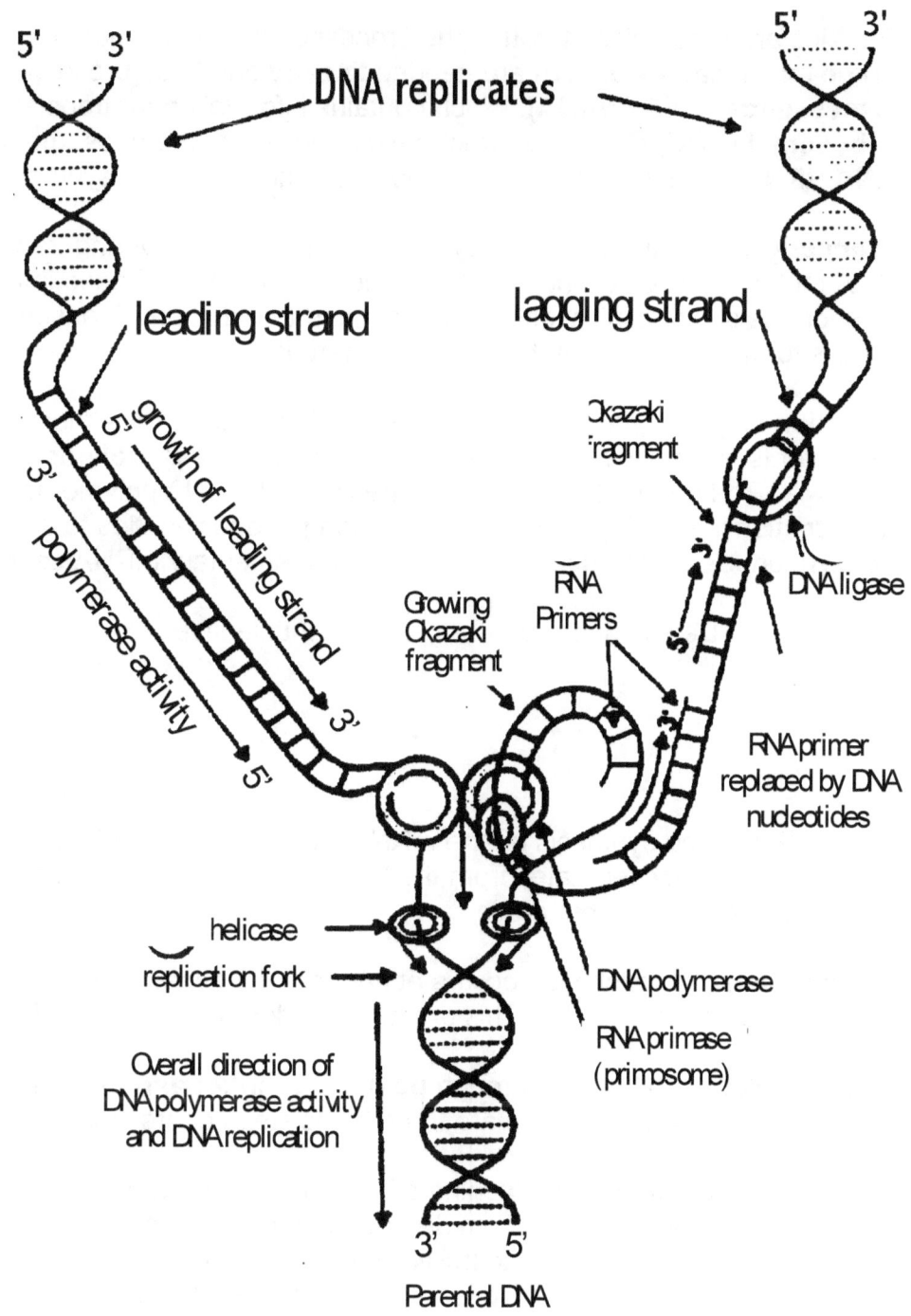

Skill 9.2 Protein synthesis

Proteins are synthesized through the processes of transcription and translation. Three major classes of RNA are needed to carry out these processes. The first is **messenger RNA (mRNA)**, which contains information for translation. **Ribosomal RNA (rRNA)** is a structural component of the ribosome and **transfer RNA (tRNA)** carries amino acids to the ribosome for protein synthesis.

Transcription is similar in prokaryotes and eukaryotes. During transcription, the DNA molecule is copied into an RNA molecule (mRNA). Transcription occurs through the steps of initiation, elongation, and termination. Transcription also occurs for rRNA and tRNA, but the focus here is on mRNA.

Initiation begins at the promoter of the double stranded DNA molecule. The promoter is a specific region of DNA that directs the **RNA polymerase** to bind to the DNA. The double stranded DNA opens up and RNA polymerase begins transcription in the 5' → 3' direction by pairing ribonucleotides to the deoxyribonucleotides as follows to get a complementary mRNA segment:

Deoxyribonucleotide		Ribonucleotide
A	→	U
G	→	C

Elongation is the synthesis on the mRNA strand in the 5' → 3' direction. The new mRNA rapidly separates from the DNA template and the complementary DNA strands pair together again.

Termination of transcription occurs at the end of a gene. Cleavage occurs at specific sites on the mRNA. This process is aided by termination factors.

In eukaryotes, mRNA goes through **posttranscriptional processing** before going on to translation. There are three basic steps of processing:

1. 5' capping is attaching a base with a methyl attached to it that protects 5' end from degradation and serves as the site where ribosome binds to mRNA for translation.
2. 3' polyadenylation is when about 100-300 adenines are added to the free 3' end of mRNA resulting in a poly-A-tail.
3. Introns (non-coding) are removed and the coding exons are spliced together to form the mature mRNA.

Translation is the process in which the mRNA sequence becomes a polypeptide. The mRNA sequence determines the amino acid sequence of a protein by following a pattern called the genetic code. The **genetic code** consists of triplet nucleotide combinations called **amino acids**. There are 20 amino acids mRNA codes for. Amino acids are the building blocks of protein. They are attached together by peptide bonds to form a polypeptide chain. There are 64 triplet combinations called codons. Three codons are termination codons and the remaining 61 code for amino acids.

Ribosomes are the site of translation. They contain rRNA and many proteins. Translation occurs in three steps: initiation, elongation, and termination. Initiation occurs when the methylated tRNA binds to the ribosome to form a complex. This complex then binds to the 5' cap of the mRNA. In elongation, tRNAs carry the amino acid to the ribosome and place it in order according to the mRNA sequence. tRNA is very specific – it only accepts one of the 20 amino acids that corresponds to the anticodon. The anticodon is complementary to the codon. For example, using the codon sequence below:

the mRNA reads A U G / G A G / C A U / G C U
the anticodons are U A C / C U C / G U A / C G A

Termination occurs when the ribosome reaches any one of the stop codons : UAA, UAG, or UGA. The newly formed polypeptide then undergoes posttranslational modification to alter or remove portions of the polypeptide.

Skill 9.3 Mutations in DNA molecules and their effect on protein structure and function

Inheritable changes in DNA are called mutations. **Mutations** may be errors in replication or a spontaneous rearrangement of one or more segments by factors like radioactivity, drugs, or chemicals. The severity of the change is not as critical as where the change occurs. DNA contains large segments of non-coding areas called introns. The important coding areas are called exons. If an error occurs on an intron, there is no effect. If the error occurs on an exon, it may be minor to lethal depending on the severity of the mistake. Mutations may occur on somatic or sex cells. Usually the mutations on sex cells are more dangerous since they contain the basis of all information for the developing offspring. But mutations are not always bad. They are the basis of evolution and if they make a more favorable variation that enhances the organism's survival, then they are beneficial. But mutations may also lead to abnormalities and birth defects and even death. There are several types of mutations.

A **point mutation** is a mutation involving a single nucleotide or a few adjacent nucleotides. Let's suppose a normal sequence was as follows:

Normal:	A B C D E F
Duplication - one gene is repeated	A B C **C** D E F
Inversion - a segment of the sequence is flipped around	A **E D C B** F
Deletion - a gene is left out	A B C E F (D is lost)
Insertion or Translocation - a segment from another place on the DNA is stuck in the wrong place	A B C **R S** D E F
Breakage - a piece is lost	A B C (DEF is lost)

Deletion and insertion mutations that shift the reading frame are **frame shift mutations**. A **silent mutation** makes no change in the amino acid sequence, therefore it does not alter the protein function. A **missense mutation** results in an alteration in the amino acid sequence.

A mutation's effect on protein function depends on which amino acid is involved and how many are involved. The structure of a protein usually determines its function. A mutation that does not alter the structure will probably have little or no effect on the protein's function. However, a mutation that does alter the structure of a protein can severely affect protein activity is called **loss-of-function mutation**. Sickle-cell anemia and cystic fibrosis are examples of loss-of-function mutations.

Sickle-cell anemia is characterized by weakness, heart failure, joint and muscular impairment, fatigue, abdominal pain and dysfunction, impaired mental function, and eventual death. The mutation that causes this genetic disorder is a point mutation in the sixth amino acid. A normal hemoglobin molecule has glutamic acid as the sixth amino acid and the sickle-cell hemoglobin has valine at the sixth position. This causes the chemical properties of hemoglobin to change. The hemoglobin of a sickle-cell person has a lower affinity for oxygen, and that causes red blood cells to have a sickle shape. The sickle shape of the red blood cell does not allow the cells to pass through capillaries well, forming clogs.

Cystic fibrosis is the most common genetic disorder of people with European ancestry. This disorder affects the exocrine system. A fibrous cyst is formed on the pancreas that blocks the pancreatic ducts. This causes sweat glands to release high levels of salt. A thick mucous is secreted from mucous glands that accumulates in the lungs. This accumulation of mucous causes bacterial infections and possibly death. Cystic fibrosis cannot be cured but can be treated for a short while. Most children with the disorder die before adulthood. Scientists identified a protein that transports chloride ions across cell membranes. Those with cystic fibrosis have a mutation in the gene coding for the protein. The majority of the mutant alleles have a deletion of the three nucleotides coding for phenylalanine at position 508. The other people with the disorder have mutant alleles caused by substitution, deletion, and frameshift mutations.

Skill 9.4 Control of gene expression in cells

In bacterial cells, the *lac* operon is a good example of the control of gene expression. The *lac* operon contains the genes that encode for the enzymes used to convert lactose into fuel (glucose and galactose). The *lac* operon contains three genes, *lac Z*, *lac Y*, and *lac A*. *Lac Z* encodes an enzyme for the conversion of lactose into glucose and galactose. *Lac Y* encodes for an enzyme that causes lactose to enter the cell. *Lac A* encodes for an enzyme that acetylates lactose.

The *lac* operon also contains a promoter and an operator that is the "off and on" switch for the operon. A protein called the repressor switches the operon off when it binds to the operator. When lactose is absent, the repressor is active and the operon is turned off. The operon is turned on again when allolactose (formed from lactose) inactivates the repressor by binding to it.

Competency 0010

Understand the procedures involved in the isolation, manipulation, and expression of genetic material and the application of genetic engineering in basic and applied research.

Skill 10.1 Understand the role of genetic engineering in the medical field

Genetic engineering has made enormous contributions to medicine. Genetic engineering has opened the door to DNA technology. The use of DNA probes and polymerase chain reaction (PCR) has enabled scientists to identify and detect elusive pathogens. Diagnosis of genetic disease is now possible before the onset of symptoms.

Genetic engineering has allowed for the treatment of some genetic disorders. **Gene therapy** is the introduction of a normal allele to the somatic cells to replace the defective allele. The medical field has had success in treating patients with a single enzyme deficiency disease. Gene therapy has allowed doctors and scientists to introduce a normal allele that would provide the missing enzyme.

Insulin and mammalian growth hormones have been produced in bacteria by gene- splicing techniques. Insulin treatment helps control diabetes for millions of people who suffer from the disease. The insulin produced in genetically engineered bacteria is chemically identical to that made in the pancreas. Human grown hormone (HGH) has been genetically engineered for treatment of dwarfism caused by insufficient amounts of HGH. HGH is being further researched for treatment of broken bones and severe burns.

Biotechnology has advanced the techniques used to create vaccines. Genetic engineering allows for the modification of a pathogen in order to attenuate it for vaccine use. In fact, vaccines created by a pathogen attenuated by gene-splicing may be safer than using the traditional mutants.

Forensic scientists regularly use DNA technology to solve crimes. DNA testing can determine a person's guilt or innocence. A suspect's DNA fingerprint is compared to the DNA found at the crime scene. If the fingerprints match, guilt can then be established.

Skill 10.2 Knowledge of genetic engineering techniques

In its simplest form, genetic engineering requires enzymes to cut DNA, a vector, and a host organism for the recombinant DNA. A **restriction enzyme** is a bacterial enzyme that cuts foreign DNA in specific locations. The restriction fragment that results can be inserted into a bacterial plasmid **(vector)**. Other vectors that may be used include viruses and bacteriophage. The splicing of restriction fragments into a plasmid results in a recombinant plasmid. This recombinant plasmid can now be placed in a host cell, usually a bacterial cell, and replicate.

The use of recombinant DNA provides a means to transplant genes among species. This opens the door for cloning specific genes of interest. Hybridization can be used to find a gene of interest. A probe is a molecule complementary in sequence to the gene of interest. The probe, once it has bonded to the gene, can be detected by labeling with a radioactive isotope or a fluorescent tag.

Gel electrophoresis is another method for analyzing DNA. Electrophoresis separates DNA or protein by size or electrical charge. The DNA runs towards the positive charge as it separates the DNA fragments by size. The gel is treated with a DNA-binding dye that fluoresces under ultraviolet light. A picture of the gel can be taken and used for analysis.

One of the most widely used genetic engineering techniques is **polymerase chain reaction (PCR)**. PCR is a technique in which a piece of DNA can be amplified into billions of copies within a few hours. This process requires primer to specify the segment to be copied, and an enzyme (usually taq polymerase) to amplify the DNA. PCR has allowed scientists to perform several procedures on the smallest amount of DNA.

Competency 0011

Understand the cell cycle, the stages and end products of meiosis and mitosis, and the role of cell division in unicellular and multicellular organisms.

Skill 11.1 Knowledge of cell division

The purpose of cell division is to provide growth and repair in body (somatic) cells and to replenish or create sex cells for reproduction. There are two forms of cell division. **Mitosis** is the division of somatic cells and **meiosis** is the division of sex cells (eggs and sperm).

Mitosis is divided into two parts: the **mitotic (M) phase** and **interphase**. In the mitotic phase, mitosis and cytokinesis divide the nucleus and cytoplasm, respectively. This phase is the shortest phase of the cell cycle. Interphase is the stage where the cell grows and copies the chromosomes in preparation for the mitotic phase. Interphase occurs in three stages of growth: **G1** (growth) period is when the cell is growing and metabolizing, the **S** period (synthesis) is where new DNA is being made and the **G2** phase (growth) is where new proteins and organelles are being made to prepare for cell division.

The mitotic phase is a continuum of change, although it is described as occurring in five stages: prophase, prometaphase, metaphase, anaphase, and telophase. During **prophase**, the cell proceeds through the following steps continuously, with no stopping. The chromatin condenses to become visible chromosomes. The nucleolus disappears and the nuclear membrane breaks apart. Mitotic spindles form that will eventually pull the chromosomes apart. They are composed of microtubules. The cytoskeleton breaks down and the spindles are pushed to the poles or opposite ends of the cell by the action of centrioles. During **prometaphase**, the nuclear membrane fragments and allows the spindle microtubules to interact with the chromosomes. Kinetochore fibers attach to the chromosomes at the centromere region. (Sometimes prometaphase is grouped with metaphase). When the centrosomes are at opposite ends of the cell, the division is in **metaphase**. The centromeres of all the chromosomes are aligned with one another. During **anaphase**, the centromeres split in half and homologous chromosomes separate. The chromosomes are pulled to the poles of the cell, with identical sets at either end. The last stage of mitosis is **telophase**. Here, two nuclei form with a full set of DNA that is identical to the parent cell. The nucleoli become visible and the nuclear membrane reassembles. A cell plate is seen in plant cells, whereas a cleavage furrow is formed in animal cells. The cell is pinched into two cells. Cytokinesis, or division of the cytoplasm and organelles, occurs.

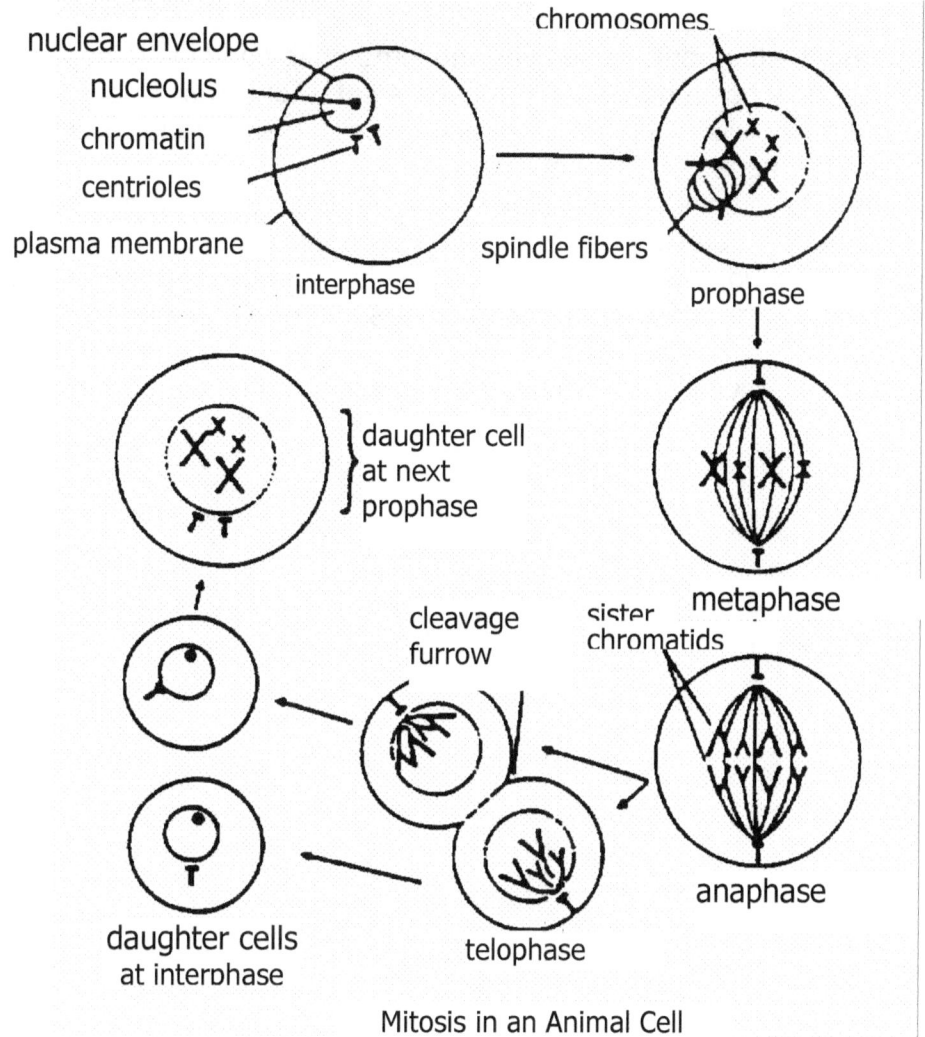

Mitosis in an Animal Cell

Meiosis is similar to mitosis, but there are two consecutive cell divisions, meiosis I and meiosis II in order to reduce the chromosome number by one half. This way, when the sperm and egg join during fertilization, the haploid number is reached.

Similar to mitosis, meiosis is preceded by an interphase during which the chromosome replicates. The steps of meiosis are as follows:

1. **Prophase I** – the replicated chromosomes condense and pair with homologues in a process called synapsis. This forms a tetrad. Crossing over, the exchange of genetic material between homologues to further increase diversity, occurs during prophase I.

2. **Metaphase I** – the homologous pairs attach to spindle fibers after lining up in the middle of the cell.
3. **Anaphase I** – the sister chromatids remain joined and move to the poles of the cell.
4. **Telophase I** – the homologous chromosome pairs continue to separate. Each pole now has a haploid chromosome set. Telophase I occurs simultaneously with cytokinesis. In animal cells, cleavage furrows form and cell plate appear in plant cells.
5. **Prophase II** – a spindle apparatus forms and the chromosomes condense.
6. **Metaphase II** – sister chromatids line up in center of cell. The centromeres divide and the sister chromatids begin to separate.
7. **Anaphase II** – the separated chromosomes move to opposite ends of the cell.
8. **Telophase II** – cytokinesis occurs, resulting in four haploid daughter cells.

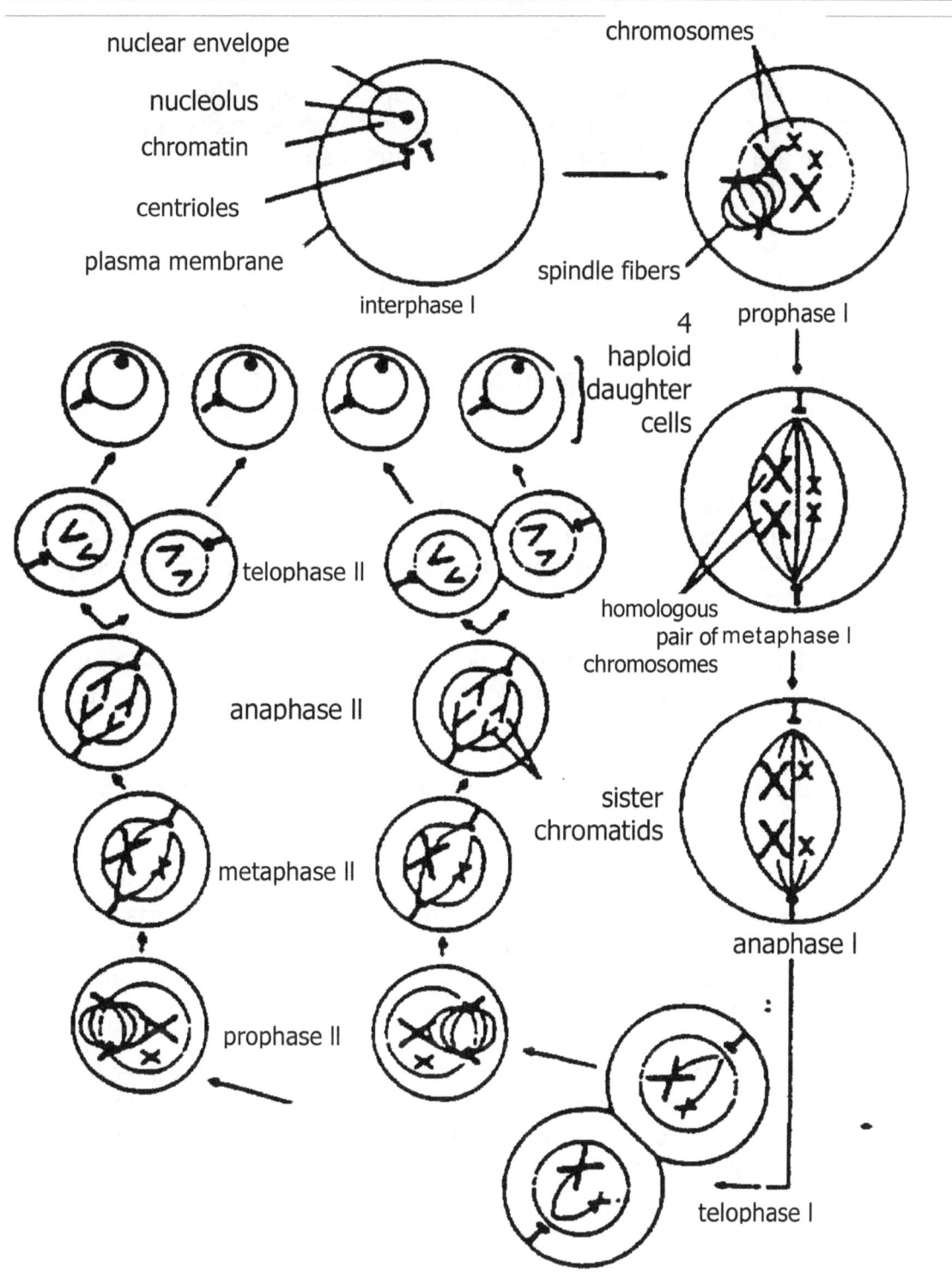

Skill 11.2 Understand genetic diversity

Meiosis and fertilization are responsible for genetic diversity. There are several mechanisms that contribute to genetic variation in sexual reproductive organisms. Three of them are independent assortment of chromosomes, crossing over, and random fertilization.

At the metaphase I stage of meiosis, each homologous pair of chromosomes is situated along the metaphase plate. The orientation of the homologous pair is random and independent of the other pairs of metaphase I. This results in an **independent assortment** of maternal and paternal chromosomes. Based on this information, it seems as though each chromosome in a gamete would be of only maternal or paternal origin. A process called crossing over prevents this from happening.

Crossing over occurs during prophase I. At this point, nonsister chromatids cross and exchange corresponding segments. Crossing over results in the combination of DNA from both parents, allowing for greater genetic variation in sexual life cycles.

Random fertilization gives way to genetic variation. Each parent has about 8 million possible chromosome combinations. This allows for over 60 trillion diploid combinations.

Skill 11.3 Understand the relationship between an unrestricted cell cycle and cancer

The restriction point occurs late in the G_1 phase of the cell cycle. This is when the decision for the cell to divide is made. If all the internal and external cell systems are working properly, the cell proceeds to replicate. Cells may also decide not to proceed past the restriction point. This nondividing cell state is called the G_0 phase. Many specialized cells remain in this state.

The density of cells also regulates cell division. Density-dependent inhibition is when the cells crowd one another and consume all the nutrients, therefore halting cell division. Cancer cells do not respond to density-dependent inhibition. They divide excessively and invade other tissues. As long as there are nutrients, cancer cells are "immortal."

Competency 0012

Understand concepts, principles, and applications of classical and molecular genetics.

Skill 12.1 Understand the basic principles of heredity

Gregor Mendel is recognized as the father of genetics. His work in the late 1800s is the basis of our knowledge of genetics. Although unaware of the presence of DNA or genes, Mendel realized there were factors (now known as **genes**) that were transferred from parents to their offspring. Mendel worked with pea plants and fertilized the plants himself, keeping track of subsequent generations which led to the Mendelian laws of genetics. Mendel found that two "factors" governed each trait, one from each parent. Traits or characteristics came in several forms, known as **alleles**. For example, the trait of flower color had white alleles (*pp*) and purple alleles (*PP*). Mendel formed two laws: the law of segregation and the law of independent assortment.

The **law of segregation** states that only one of the two possible alleles from each parent is passed on to the offspring. If the two alleles differ, then one is fully expressed in the organism's appearance (the dominant allele) and the other has no noticeable effect on appearance (the recessive allele). The two alleles for each trait segregate into different gametes. A Punnet square can be used to show the law of segregation. In a Punnet square, one parent's genes are put at the top of the box and the other parent's on the side. Genes combine in the squares just like numbers are added in addition tables. This Punnet square shows the result of the cross of two F_1 hybrids.

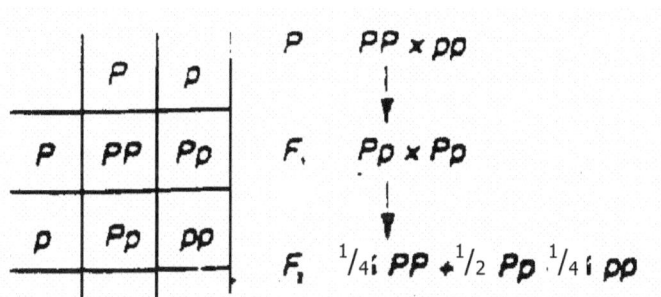

This cross results in a 1:2:1 ratio of F_2 offspring. Here, the *P* is the dominant allele and the *p* is the recessive allele. The F_1 cross produces three offspring with the dominant allele expressed (two *PP* and *Pp*) and one offspring with the recessive allele expressed (*pp*). Some other important terms to know:

> **Homozygous** – having a pair of identical alleles. For example, *PP* and *pp* are homozygous pairs.
> **Heterozygous** – having two different alleles. For example, *Pp* is a heterozygous pair.

Phenotype – the organism's physical appearance.
Genotype – the organism's genetic makeup. For example, *PP* and *Pp* have the same phenotype (purple in color), but different genotypes.

The **law of independent assortment** states that alleles sort independently of each other. The law of segregation applies for a monohybrid crosses (only one character, in this case flower color, is experimented with). In a dihybrid cross, two characters are being explored. Two of the seven characters Mendel studied were seed shape and color. Yellow is the dominant seed color (*Y*) and green is the recessive color (*y*). The dominant seed shape is round (*R*) and the recessive shape is wrinkled (*r*). A cross between a plant with yellow round seeds (*YYRR*) and a plant with green wrinkled seeds (*yyrr*) produces an F_1 generation with the genotype *YyRr*. The production of F_2 offspring results in a 9:3:3:1 phenotypic ratio.

F_2

	YR	Yr	yR	yr
YR	YYRR	YYRr	YyRR	YyRr
Yr	YYRr	YYrr	YyRr	Yyrr
yR	YyRR	YyRr	yyRR	yyRr
yr	YyRr	Yyrr	yyRr	yyrr

P   YYRR × yyrr
↓
F_1 YyRr
↓
F_2 YYRR - 1 ⎫
        YYRr - 2 ⎬ 9 yellow round
        YyRR - 2 ⎪
        YyRr - 4 ⎭

        yyRR - 1 ⎫ 3 green round
        yyRr - 2 ⎭

        YYrr - 1 ⎫ 3 yellow wrinkled
        Yyrr - 2 ⎭

        yyrr - 1 } 1 green wrinkled

Based on Mendelian genetics, the more complex hereditary pattern of **dominance** was discovered. In Mendel's law of segregation, the F_1 generation have either purple or white flowers. This is an example of **complete dominance**. **Incomplete dominance** is when the F_1 generation results in an appearance somewhere between the two parents. For example, red flowers are crossed with white flowers, resulting in an F_1 generation with pink flowers. The red and white traits are still carried by the F_1 generation, resulting in an F_2 generation with a phenotypic ration of 1:2:1. In **codominance,** the genes may form new phenotypes. The ABO blood grouping is an example of codominance. A and B are of equal strength and O is recessive. Therefore, type A blood may have the genotypes of AA or AO, type B blood may have the genotypes of BB or BO, type AB blood has the genotype A and B, and type O blood has two recessive O genes.

Skill 12.2 Analyzing genetic inheritance problems

The same techniques of pedigree analysis apply when tracing inherited disorders. Thousands of genetic disorders are the result of inheriting a recessive trait. These disorders range from nonlethal traits (such as albinism) to life-threatening (such as cystic fibrosis).

Most people with recessive disorders are born to parents with normal phenotypes. The mating of heterozygous parents would result in an offspring genotypic ratio of 1:2:1; thus 1 out of 4 offspring would express this recessive trait. The heterozygous parents are called carriers because they do not express the trait phenotypically but pass the trait on to their offspring.

Lethal dominant alleles are much less common than lethal recessives. This is because lethal dominant alleles are not masked in heterozygotes. Mutations in a gene of the sperm or egg can result in a lethal dominant allele, usually killing the developing offspring.

Sex linked traits - the Y chromosome found only in males (XY) carries very little genetic information, whereas the X chromosome found in females (XX) carries very important information. Since men have no second X chromosome to cover up a recessive gene, the recessive trait is expressed more often in men. Women need the recessive gene on both X chromosomes to show the trait. Examples of sex linked traits include hemophilia and color-blindness.

Sex influenced traits - traits are influenced by the sex hormones. Male pattern baldness is an example of a sex influenced trait. Testosterone influences the expression of the gene. Mostly men loose their hair due to this.

Nondisjunction - during meiosis, chromosomes fail to separate properly. One sex cell may get both chromosomes and another may get none. Depending on the chromosomes involved this may or may not be serious. Offspring end up with either an extra chromosome or are missing one. An example of nondisjunction is Down Syndrome, where three #21 chromosomes are present.

Chromosome Theory - Noted by Walter Sutton in the early 1900's. In the late 1800's, the processes of mitosis and meiosis were now understood. Sutton saw how this explanation confirmed Mendel's "factors". The chromosome theory basically states that genes are located on chromosomes. The chromosomes undergo independent assortment and segregation.

Skill 12.3 Analyze the techniques used to screen for genetic disorders

Some genetic disorders can be prevented. The parents can be screened for genetic disorders before the child is conceived or in the early stages of pregnancy. Genetic counselors determine the risk of producing offspring that may express a genetic disorder. The counselor reviews the family's pedigree and determines the frequency of a recessive allele. While genetic counseling is helpful for future parents, there is no certainty in the outcome.

There are some genetic disorders that can be discovered in a heterozygous parent. For example, sickle-cell anemia and cystic fibrosis alleles can be discovered in carriers by genetic testing. If the parents are carriers but decide to have children anyway, fetal testing is available during the pregnancy. There are a few techniques available to determine if a developing fetus will have the genetic disorder.

Amniocentesis is a procedure in which a needle is inserted into the uterus to extract some of the amniotic fluid surrounding the fetus. Some disorders can be detected by chemicals in the fluid. Other disorders can be detected by karyotyping cells cultured from the fluid to identify certain chromosomal defects.

A physician removes some of the fetal tissue from the placenta in a technique called **chorionic villus sampling (CVS)**. The cells are then karyotyped as they are in amniocentesis. The advantage of CVS is that the cells can be karyotyped immediately, unlike in amniocentesis which take several weeks to culture.

Unlike amniocentesis and CVS, **ultrasounds** are a non-invasive technique for detecting genetic disorders. Ultrasound can only detect physical abnormalities of the fetus.

Newborn screening is now routinely performed in the United States at birth. Phenylketonuria (PKU) is a recessively inherited disorder that does not allow children to properly break down the amino acid phenylalanine. This amino acid and its by-product accumulate in the blood to toxic levels, resulting in mental retardation. This can be prevented by screening at birth for this defect and treating it with a special diet.

Skill 12.4 Understand the role of nonnuclear inheritance

Mitochondrial DNA is passed to the next generation by the mother. A genetic defect in the mother's mitochondrial DNA will pass to her offspring, regardless of the paternal DNA.

Competency 0013

Understand the principles of population genetics and the interaction between heredity and the environment, and apply this knowledge to problems involving populations.

Skill 13.1 Analyze the conditions that affect the gene pool

Evolution currently is defined as a change in genotype over time. Gene frequencies shift and change from generation to generation. Populations evolve, not individuals. The **Hardy-Weinberg** theory of gene equilibrium is a mathematical prediction to show shifting gene patterns. Let's use the letter "A" to represent the dominant condition of normal skin pigment. "a" would represent the recessive condition of albinism. In a population, there are three possible genotypes; AA, Aa and aa. AA and Aa would have normal skin pigment and only aa would be albinos. According to the Hardy-Weinberg law, there are five requirements to keep a gene frequency stable, leading to no evolution:

1. There is no mutation in the population.
2. There are no selection pressures; one gene is not more desirable in the environment.
3. There is no mating preference; mating is random.
4. The population is isolated; there is no immigration or emigration.
5. The population is large (mathematical probability is more correct with a large sample).

The above conditions are extremely difficult to meet. If these five conditions are not met, then gene frequency can shift, leading to evolution. Let's say in a population, 75% of the population has normal skin pigment (AA and Aa) and 25% are albino (aa). Using the following formula, we can determine the frequency of the A allele and the "a" allele in a population.

This can be used over generations to determine if evolution is occurring. The formula is: $1 = p^2 + 2pq + q^2$; where 1 is the total population. p^2 is the number of AA individuals, 2pq is the number of Aa individuals, and q^2 is the number of aa individuals.

Since you cannot tell by looking if an individual is AA or Aa, you must use the aa individuals to find that frequency first. As stated above aa was 25% of the population. Since $aa = q^2$, we can determine the value of q (or a) by finding the square root of 0.25, which is 0.5. Therefore, 0.5 of the population has the "a" gene. In order to find the value for p, use the following formula: $1 = p + q$. This would make the value of $p = 0.5$.

BIOLOGICAL SCIENCES

The gene pool is all the alleles at all gene loci in all individuals of a population. The Hardy-Weinberg theorem describes the gene pool in a non-evolving population. It states that the frequencies of alleles and genotypes in a population's gene pool are random unless acted on by something other than sexual recombination.

Now, to find the number of AA, plug it into the first formula;
$AA = p^2 = 0.5 \times 0.5 = 0.25$

$Aa = 2pq = 2(0.5 \times 0.5) = 0.5$
$aa = q^2 = 0.5 \times 0.5 = 0.25$

Any problem you may have with Hardy Weinberg will have an obvious squared number. The square of that number will be the frequency of the recessive gene, and you can figure anything else out knowing the formula and the frequency of q!

When frequencies vary from the Hardy Weinberg equilibrium, the population is said to be evolving. The change to the gene pool is on such a small scale that it is called microevolution. Certain factors increase the chances of variability in a population, thus leading to evolution. Items that increase variability include mutations, sexual reproduction, immigration, large population, and variation in geographic local. Changes that decrease variation would be natural selection, emigration, small population, and random mating.

Skill 13.2 Recognize the relationship between phenotype and its selective advantage in the environment

The environment can have an impact on phenotype. For example, a person living in a higher altitude will have a varying amount of red and white blood cells than those living at sea level.
In some cases, a particular trait is advantageous to the organism in a particular environment. Sickle-cell disease causes a low oxygen level in the blood which results in red blood cells having a sickle shape. About one in every ten African-Americans have the sickle-cell trait. These heterozygous carriers are usually healthy compared to homozygous individuals who can suffer severe detrimental effects. In the tropical Africa environment, a heterozygote is more resistant to malaria than those who do not carry any copies of the sickle-cell gene.

Competency 0014

Understand the processes of natural selection and adaptation and evolutionary theory.

Skill 14.1 Analyze the role of natural selection on evolution

Natural selection is based on the survival of certain traits in a population through the course of time. The phrase "survival of the fittest," is often associated with natural selection. Fitness is the contribution an individual makes to the gene pool of the next generation.

Natural selection acts on phenotypes. An organism's phenotype is constantly exposed to its environment. Based on an organism's phenotype, selection indirectly adapts a population to its environment by maintaining favorable genotypes in the gene pool.

There are three modes of natural selection. Stabilizing selection favors the more common phenotypes, directional selection shifts the frequency of phenotypes in one direction, and diversifying selection occurs when individuals on both extremes of the phenotypic range are favored.

Sexual selection leads to the secondary sex characteristics between male and females. Animals that use mating behaviors may be successful or unsuccessful. An animal that lacks attractive plumage or has a weak mating call will not attract the female, thereby eventually limiting that gene in the gene pool. Mechanical isolation, where sex organs do not fit the female, has an obvious disadvantage.

Skill 14.2 Compare alternative mechanisms of evolution

There are two theories on the rate of evolution. **Gradualism** is the theory that minor evolutionary changes occur at a regular rate. Darwin's book, "On the Origin of Species," is based on this theory of gradualism. Charles Darwin was born in 1809 and spent 5 years in his twenties on a ship called the *Beagle*. Of all the locations the *Beagle* sailed to, it was the Galapagos Islands that infatuated Darwin. There he collected 13 species of finches that were quite similar. He could not accurately determine whether these finches were of the same species. He later learned these finches were in fact separate species. Darwin began to hypothesize that new species arose from its ancestors by the gradual collection of adaptations to a different environment. Darwin's most popular hypothesis is on the beak size of Galapagos finches. He theorized that the finches' beak sizes evolved to accommodate different food sources. Many people did not believe in Darwin's theories until recent field studies proved successful.

Although Darwin believed the origin of species was gradual, he was bewildered by the gaps in fossil records of living organisms. **Punctuated equilibrium** is the model of evolution that states that organismal form diverges and species form rapidly over relatively short periods of geological history, and then progress through long stages of stasis with little or no change. Punctuationalists use fossil records to support their claim. It is probable that both theories are correct, depending on the particular lineage studied.

Skill 14.3 Recognize the factors that lead to speciation

The most commonly used species concept is the **Biological Species Concept (BSC)**. This states that a species is a reproductive community of populations that occupy a specific niche in nature. It focuses on reproductive isolation of populations as the primary criterion for recognition of species status. The biological species concept does not apply to organisms that are completely asexual in their reproduction, fossil organisms, or distinctive populations that hybridize.

Reproductive isolation is caused by any factor that impedes two species from producing viable, fertile hybrids. Reproductive barriers can be categorized as **prezygotic** (premating) or **postzygotic** (postmating).

The prezygotic barriers are as follows:

1. Habitat isolation – species occupy different habitats in the same territory.
2. Temporal isolation – populations reaching sexual maturity/flowering at different times of the year.
3. Ethological isolation – behavioral differences that reduce or prevent interbreeding between individuals of different species (including pheromones and other attractants).
4. Mechanical isolation – structural differences that make gamete transfer difficult or impossible.
5. Gametic isolation – male and female gametes do not attract each other; no fertilization.

The postzygotic barriers are as follows:

1. Hybrid inviability – hybrids die before sexual maturity.
2. Hybrid sterility – disrupts gamete formation; no normal sex cells.
3. Hybrid breakdown – reduces viability or fertility in progeny of the F_2 backcross.

Geographical isolation can also lead to the origin of species. **Allopatric speciation** is speciation without geographic overlap. It is the accumulation of genetic differences through division of a species' range, either through a physical barrier separating the population or through expansion by dispersal such that gene flow is cut. In **sympatric speciation**, new species arise within the range of parent populations. Populations are sympatric if their geographical range overlaps. This usually involves the rapid accumulation of genetic differences (usually chromosomal rearrangements) that prevent interbreeding with adjacent populations.

Skill 14.4 Evaluate observations made in various areas of biology (e.g., embryology, biochemistry, anatomy) in terms of evolutionary theory

1. Embryology:
Comparative embryology shows how embryos start off looking the same. As they develop, their similarities slowly decrease until they take the form of their particular class.

For example, adult vertebrates are diverse, yet their embryos are quite similar at very early stages. Fish like structures still form in early embryos of reptiles, birds, and mammals. In fish embryos, a two chambered heart, some veins, and parts of arteries develop and persist in adult fishes. The same structures form early in human embryos but do not persist as such in adults.

2. Biochemistry:
All known extant organisms make use of DNA and /or RNA. ATP is used as metabolic currency by all extant life. The genetic code is same for all organisms, meaning that a piece of RNA in a bacterium codes for the same protein as in a human cell.

A classic example of biochemical evidence for evolution is the variance of the protein Cytochrome c in living cells. The variance of Cytochrome c of different organisms is measured in the number of differing amino acids, each differing amino acid being a result of a base pair substitution, a mutation. If each differing amino acid is assumed to be the result of one base pair substitution, it can be calculated how long ago the two species diverged by multiplying the number of base pair substitutions by the estimated time it takes for a substituted base pair of the Cytochrome c gene to mutate in N thousand years, the number of amino acids making up the Cytochrome c protein in monkeys differ by one from that of humans, this leads us to believe that the two species diverged N million years ago.

3. Anatomy:

Comparative study of the anatomy of the groups of animals or plants reveals that certain structural features are basically similar. For example, the basic structure of all flowers sepals, petals, stigma, style and ovary; yet the size, color, number of parts and specific structure are different for each individual species. The degree of resemblance between to organisms should indicate how closely related they are in evolution.

* Groups with little in common are assumed to have diverged from a common ancestor much earlier in geological history than groups which have a lot in common.

* In deciding how closely related two animals are, a comparative anatomist looks for structures which, though they may serve quite different functions in the adult, are fundamentally similar, suggesting a common origin. Such structures are described as homologous; and

* In cases where the similar structures serve different functions in adults, it may be necessary to trace their origin and embryonic development, to look for more similarities derived from a common ancestor.

Competency 0015

Understand the principles of taxonomy.

Skill 15.1 Knowledge of the classification of organisms

It is believed that there are probably over ten million different species of living things. Of these, 1.5 million have been named and classified. Systems of classification show similarities and also assist scientists with a world wide system of organization.

Carolus Linnaeus is termed the father of taxonomy. **Taxonomy** is the science of classification. Linnaeus based his system on morphology (study of structure). Later on, evolutionary relationships (phylogeny) were also used to sort and group species. The modern classification system uses binomial nomenclature. This consists of a two word name for every species. The genus is the first part of the name and the species is the second part. Notice in the levels explained below that Homo sapiens is the scientific name for humans. Starting with the kingdom, the groups get smaller and more alike as one moves down the levels in the classification of humans:

Kingdom: Animalia, Phylum: Chordata, Subphylum: Vertebrata, Class: Mammalia, Order: Primate, Family: Hominidae, Genus: Homo, Species: sapiens

Species are defined by the ability to successfully reproduce with members of their own kind.

Several different morphological criteria are used to classify organisms:

1. **Ancestral characters** - characteristics that are unchanged after evolution (ie: 5 digits on the hand of an ape).

2. **Derived characters** - characteristics that have evolved more recently (ie: the absence of a tail on an ape).

3. **Conservative characters** - traits that change slowly.

4. **Homologous characters** - characteristics with the same genetic basis but used for a different function. (ie: wing of a bat, arm of a human. The bone structure is the same, but the limbs are used for different purposes).

5. **Analogous characters** – structures that differ, but used for similar purposes (ie- the wing of a bird and the wing of a butterfly).

6. **Convergent evolution** - development of similar adaptations by organisms that are unrelated.

Biological characteristics are also used to classify organisms. Protein comparison, DNA comparison, and analysis of fossilized DNA are powerful comparative methods used to measure evolutionary relationships between species. Taxonomists consider the organism's life history, biochemical (DNA) makeup, behavior, and how the organisms are distributed geographically. The fossil record is also used to show evolutionary relationships.

Skill 15.2 Analyzing a phylogenetic tree or cladogram of related species

The typical graphic product of a classification is a **phylogenetic tree**, which represents a hypothesis of the relationships based on branching of lineages through time within a group. Every time you see a phylogenetic tree, you should be aware that it is making statements on the degree of similarity between organisms, or the particular pattern in which the various lineages diverged (phylogenetic history).

Cladistics is the study of phylogenetic relationships of organisms by analysis of shared, derived character states. Cladograms are constructed to show evolutionary pathways. Character states are polarized in cladistic analysis to be plesiomorphous (ancestral features), symplesiomorphous (shared ancestral features), apomorphous (derived characteristics), and synapomorphous (shared, derived features).

Skill 15.3 Analyzing the impact of evolution and modern genetics in the classification system

The current five kingdom system separates prokaryotes from eukaryotes. The prokaryotes belong to the kingdom monera while the eukaryotes belong to either kingdom protista, plantae, fungi, or animalia. Recent comparisons of nucleic acids and proteins between different groups of organisms have led to problems concerning the five kingdom system. Based on these comparisons, alternative kingdom systems have emerged. Six and eight kingdoms as well as a three domain system have been proposed as a more accurate classification system. It is important to note that classification systems evolve as more information regarding characteristics and evolutionary histories of organisms arise.

Competency 0016

Understand the unity and diversity of life, including common structures and functions.

Skill 16.1 Knowledge of the properties of life

Life has defining properties. Some of the more important processes and properties associated with life are as follows:

- Order – an organism's complex organization.
- Reproduction – life only comes from life (biogenesis).
- Energy utilization – organisms use and make energy to do many kinds of work.
- Growth and development – DNA directed growth and development.
- Adaptation to the environment – occurs by homeostasis (ability to maintain a certain status), response to stimuli, and evolution.

Skill 16.2 Recognize the levels of organization

Life is highly organized. The organization of living systems builds on levels from small to increasingly more large and complex. All aspects, whether it is a cell or an ecosystem, have the same requirements to sustain life. Life is organized from simple to complex in the following way:

Atoms→molecules→organelles→cells→tissues→organs→organ systems→organism

Skill 16.3 Comparing and analyzing the basic life functions carried out by living organisms (e.g., obtaining nutrients, excretion, reproduction)

Members of the five different kingdoms of the classification system of living organisms often differ in their basic life functions. Here we compare and analyze how members of the five kingdoms obtain nutrients, excrete waste, and reproduce.

Bacteria are prokaryotic, single-celled organisms that lack cell nuclei. The different types of bacteria obtain nutrients in a variety of ways. Most bacteria absorb nutrients from the environment through small channels in their cell walls and membranes (chemotrophs) while some perform photosynthesis (phototrophs). Chemoorganotrophs use organic compounds as energy sources while chemolithotrophs can use inorganic chemicals as energy sources. Depending on the type of metabolism and energy source, bacteria release a variety of waste products (e.g. alcohols, acids, carbon dioxide) to the environment through diffusion.

All bacteria reproduce through binary fission (asexual reproduction) producing two identical cells. Bacteria reproduce very rapidly, dividing or doubling every twenty minutes in optimal conditions. Asexual reproduction does not allow for genetic variation, but bacteria achieve genetic variety by absorbing DNA from ruptured cells and conjugating or swapping chromosomal or plasmid DNA with other cells.

Animals are multicellular, eukaryotic organisms. All animals obtain nutrients by eating food (ingestion). Different types of animals derive nutrients from eating plants, other animals, or both. Animal cells perform respiration that converts food molecules, mainly carbohydrates and fats, into energy. The excretory systems of animals, like animals themselves, vary in complexity. Simple invertebrates eliminate waste through a single tube, while complex vertebrates have a specialized system of organs that process and excrete waste.

Most animals, unlike bacteria, exist in two distinct sexes. Members of the female sex give birth or lay eggs. Some less developed animals can reproduce asexually. For example, flatworms can divide in two and some unfertilized insect eggs can develop into viable organisms. Most animals reproduce sexually through various mechanisms. For example, aquatic animals reproduce by external fertilization of eggs, while mammals reproduce by internal fertilization. More developed animals possess specialized reproductive systems and cycles that facilitate reproduction and promote genetic variation.

Plants, like animals, are multi-cellular, eukaryotic organisms. Plants obtain nutrients from the soil through their root systems and convert sunlight into energy through photosynthesis. Many plants store waste products in vacuoles or organs (e.g. leaves, bark) that are discarded. Some plants also excrete waste through their roots.

More than half of the plant species reproduce by producing seeds from which new plants grow. Depending on the type of plant, flowers or cones produce seeds. Other plants reproduce by spores, tubers, bulbs, buds, and grafts. The flowers of flowering plants contain the reproductive organs. Pollination is the joining of male and female gametes that is often facilitated by movement by wind or animals.

Fungi are eukaryotic, mostly multi-cellular organisms. All fungi are heterotrophs, obtaining nutrients from other organisms. More specifically, most fungi obtain nutrients by digesting and absorbing nutrients from dead organisms. Fungi secrete enzymes outside of their body to digest organic material and then absorb the nutrients through their cell walls.

Most fungi can reproduce asexually and sexually. Different types of fungi reproduce asexually by mitosis, budding, sporification, or fragmentation. Sexual reproduction of fungi is different from sexual reproduction of animals. The two mating types of fungi are plus and minus, not male and female. The fusion of hyphae, the specialized reproductive structure in fungi, between plus and minus types produces and scatters diverse spores.

Protists are eukaryotic, single-celled organisms. Most protists are heterotrophic, obtaining nutrients by ingesting small molecules and cells and digesting them in vacuoles. All protists reproduce asexually by either binary or multiple fission. Like bacteria, protists achieve genetic variation by exchange of DNA through conjugation.

Skill 16.4 Recognize the importance of maintaining biological diversity (e.g., pharmacological products, stability of ecosystems).

Biological diversity is the extraordinary variety of living things and ecological communities interacting with each other throughout the world. Maintaining biological diversity is important for many reasons. First, we derive many consumer products used by humans from living organisms in nature. Second, the stability and habitability of the environment depends on the varied contributions of many different organisms. Finally, the cultural traditions of human populations depend on the diversity of the natural-world.

Many pharmacological products of importance to human health have their origins in nature. For example, scientists first harvested aspirin, a derivative of salicylic acid from the bark of willow trees. In addition, nature is also the source of many medicines including antibiotics, anti-malarial drugs, and cancer fighting compounds. However, scientists have yet to study the potential medicinal properties of many plant species, including the majority of rain forest plants. Thus, losing such plants to extinction may result in the loss of promising treatments for human diseases.

The basic stability of ecosystems depends on the interaction and contributions of a wide variety of species. For example, all living organisms require nitrogen to live. Only a select few species of microorganisms can convert atmospheric nitrogen into a form that is usable by most other organisms (nitrogen fixation). Thus, humans and all other organisms depend on the existence of the nitrogen-fixing microbes. In addition, the cycling of carbon, oxygen, and water depends on the contributions of many different types of plants, animals, and microorganisms. Finally, the existence and functioning of a diverse range of species creates healthy, stable ecosystems. Stable ecosystems are more adaptable and less susceptible to extreme events like floods and droughts.

Aside from its scientific value, biological diversity greatly affects human culture and cultural diversity. Human life and culture is tied to natural resources. For example, the availability of certain types of fish defines the culture of many coastal human populations. The disappearance of fish populations because of environmental disruptions changes the entire way of life of a group of people. The loss of cultural diversity, like the loss of biological diversity, diminishes the very fabric of the world population.

Skill 16.5 Analyze the processes involved in homeostasis

The molecular composition of the immediate environment outside of the organism is not the same as it is inside and the temperature outside may not be optimal for metabolic activity within the organism. **Homeostasis** is the control of these differences between internal and external environments. There are three homeostatic systems to regulate these differences.

Osmoregulation deals with maintenance of the appropriate level of water and salts in body fluids for optimum cellular functions. **Excretion** is the elimination of metabolic waste products from the body including excess water.
Thermoregulation maintains the internal, or core, body temperature of the organism within a tolerable range for metabolic and cellular processes.

Competency 0017

Understand the characteristics, functions, and adaptations of viruses, archaebacteria, monerans, protoctists (protists), and fungi.

Skill 17.1 Analyze the structure and processes of prions and viruses

Microbiology includes the study of monera, protists and viruses. Although **viruses** are not classified as living things, they greatly affect other living things by disrupting cell activity. They are considered to be obligate parasites because they rely on the host for their own reproduction. Viruses are composed of a protein coat and a nucleic acid, either DNA or RNA. A bacteriophage is a virus that infects a bacterium. Animal viruses are classified by the type of nucleic acid, presence of RNA replicase, and presence of a protein coat.

There are two types of viral reproductive cycles:

1. **Lytic cycle** - the virus enters the host cell and makes copies of its nucleic acids and protein coats and reassembles. It then lyses or breaks out of the host cell and infects other nearby cells, repeating the process.
2. **Lysogenic cycle** - the virus may remain dormant within the cells until something initiates it to break out of the cell. Herpes is an example of a lysogenic virus.

Prions are protein fibrils that contain no DNA or RNA. Prions cause scrapie in sheep and bovine spongiform encephalitis ("mad-cow" disease) in cows. This disease is characterized by a sponge-like brain. Prions cause slow developing disease of the nervous system in humans similar to those in animals. Kreutzfeldt-Jacob Syndrome and kuru are two of the human diseases caused by prions. The prion diseases are contracted by consuming the tissue of infected organisms.

Skill 17.2 Compare archaebacteria and eubacteria

Archaebacteria and eubacteria are the two main branches of prokaryotic (moneran) evolution. Archaebacteria evolved from the earliest cells. Most achaebacteria inhabit extreme environments. There are three main groups of archaebacteria. Methanogens are strict anaerobes, extreme halophiles live in high salt concentrations, and extreme thermophiles live in hot temperatures (hot springs).

Most prokaryotes fall into the eubacteria (bacteria) domain. **Bacteria** are divided according to their morphology (shape). Bacilli are rod shaped bacteria, cocci are round bacteria and spirilli are spiral shaped.

The Gram stain is a procedure used to differentiate the cell wall make-up of bacteria. Gram positive bacteria have simple cell walls consisting of large amounts of peptidoglycan. These bacteria pick up the stain, revealing a purple color when observed under the microscope. Gram negative bacteria have a more complex cell wall consisting of less peptidoglycan, but have large amounts of lipopolysaccharides. The lipopolysaccharides resist the stain, revealing a pink color when observed under the microscope. Because of the lipopolysaccharide cell wall, Gram negative bacteria tend to be more toxic and are more resistant to antibiotics and host defense mechanisms.

Bacteria reproduce by binary fission. This asexual process is simply dividing the bacterium in half. All new organisms are exact clones of the parent.

Some bacteria have a sticky capsule that protects the cell wall and is also used for adhesion to surfaces. Pili are surface appendages for adhesion to other cells.

Bacteria locomotion is via flagella or taxis. Taxis is the movement towards or away from a stimulus. The methods for obtaining nutrition are: for photosynthetic organisms or producers- the conversion of sunlight to chemical energy, consumers or heterotrophs- consuming other living organisms, and saprophytes are consumers that live off dead or decaying material.

In comparison, archaebacteria contain no peptidoglycan in the cell wall, they are not inhibited by antibiotics, they have several kinds of RNA polymerase, and they do not have a nuclear envelope. Eubacteria (bacteria) have peptidoglycan in the cell wall, they are susceptible to antibiotics, they have one kind of RNA polymerase, and they have no nuclear envelope.

Skill 17.3 Chromosome and plasmid replication in bacteria

Chromosomal replication in bacteria is similar to eukaryotic DNA replication.

A **plasmid** is a small ring of DNA that carries accessory genes separate from those of a bacterial chromosome. Most plasmids in Gram negative bacteria undergo bidirectional replication, although some replicate unidirectional because of its small size. Plasmids in Gram positive bacteria replicate by the rolling circle mechanism.

Some plasmids can transfer themselves (and therefore their genetic information) by a process called conjugation. Conjugation requires cell-cell contact. The sex pilus of the donor cell attaches to the recipient cell. Once contact has been established, the transfer of DNA occurs by the rolling circle mechanism.

Skill 17.4 Structure and function of protists

Protists are the earliest eukaryotic descendants of prokaryotes. Protists are found almost anywhere there is water. Protists can be broadly defined as the eukaryotic microorganisms and include the macroscopic algae with only a single tissue type. They are defined by exclusion of characteristics common of the other kingdoms. They are not prokaryotes because they have (usually) a true nucleus and membrane bound organelles. They are not fungi because fungi lack undulopidia and develop from spores. They are not plants because plants develop from embryos, and they are not animals because animals develop from a blastula.

Most protists have a true (membrane-bound) nucleus, complex organelles (mitochondria, chloroplasts, etc.), aerobic respiration in mitochondria, and undulipodium (cilia) in some life stage.

The chaotic status of names and concepts of the higher classification of the protists reflects their great diversity of form, function, and life cycles. The protists are often grouped as algae (plant-like), protozoa (animal-like), or fungus-like, based on the similarity of their lifestyle and characteristics to these more derived groups. Two distinctive groups of protists are considered for separation as their own kingdoms. The **Archaezoa** lack mitochondria, the Golgi apparatus, and have multiple nuclei. The **Chromista**, including diatoms, brown algae and "golden" algae with chlorophyll *c*, have a very different photosynthetic plastid from those found in the green algae and plants.

Skill 17.5 Knowledge of the significance of fungi, bacteria, and viruses

Although bacteria and fungi may cause disease, they are also beneficial for use as medicines and food. Penicillin is derived from a fungus that is capable of destroying the cell wall of bacteria. Most antibiotics work in this way. Some antibiotics can interfere with bacterial DNA replication or can disrupt the bacterial ribosome without affecting the host cells. Viral diseases have been fought through the use of vaccination, where a small amount of the virus is introduced so the immune system is able to recognize it upon later infection. Antibodies are more quickly manufactured when the host has had prior exposure.

The majority of prokaryotes decompose material for use by the environment and other organisms. The eukaryotic fungi are the most important decomposers in the biosphere. They break down organic material to be used up by other living organisms. The fungi are characterized by a short lived diploid stage, which cannot be viewed except under a microscope. The structures that are visible to the naked eye are typically puffballs, mushrooms, and shelf fungi that represent the dikaryote form of the fungi. The haploid stages are commonly observed as the absorptive hyphae or as asexual reproductive sporangia.

Skill 17.6 Analyze the process of gene transfer in monerans.

The transfer of genetic material between bacteria is known as bacterial conjugation. While this process is somewhat similar to sexual reproduction because genes are exchanged, it does not involve the fusing of gametes. Conjugation is the form of horizontal gene transfer, a process by which an organism transfers genes to another organism that is not its offspring.

In conjugation, one bacteria serves as the donor cell and the other is the recipient. The donor cell must possess a transferable genetic element, typically a plasmid. The first step of conjugation is the donor cell producing a pilus (a hairlike structure on the cell surface), which attaches to the recipient cell and draws the two cells together. The double stranded DNA of the plasmid is then nicked and a single strand of it is transferred to the recipient cell. Both cells then recircularize the DNA and synthesize a second strand.

Bacterial conjugation is usually beneficial to the recipient cell, since it often transfers a gene that gives the recipient new abilities, such as antibiotic resistance or a digestive enzyme. An example of a commonly transferred plasmid is the F-plasmid, which is an episome. An episome is a special type of plasmid that can integrate itself into the bacterial chromosome. The F-plasmid carries genes that allow a bacteria to produce pili on their surfaces as well as associated proteins and regulatory genes. Thus, by definition, any donor cell must possess the F-plasmid to produce a pili and transfer DNA via conjugation. Note that DNA transfer does not take place *through* the pili, but that a channel opens between the bacteria and the DNA passes through this channel. The genes that allow the formation of this channel are also found on the F-plasmid. Because the F-plasmid is an episome, it can sometimes carry chromosomal DNA from the donor cell to the recipient. Most conjugative plasmids, including the F-plasmid, have systems to ensure that the recipient cell does not already possess a similar element.

There are at least three other methods of horizontal gene transfer in bacteria, though they occur more rarely in nature. The first is simple fusion between bacteria. The second is transformation, which is direct uptake of free DNA or RNA by a bacterium. Transformation requires the recipient cell be made competent (permeable to free genetic material) via either natural or artificial means. The third is transduction, the introduction of bacterial DNA to another bacterium using a virus or free plasmid. However, conjugation and cell fusion necessitate cell-to-cell contact and do not require any mediating agents (virus or plasmid). The methods of transformation and transduction are most commonly used in laboratory conditions to introduce new genes into bacteria.

Competency 0018

Understand the characteristics, functions, and adaptations of plants.

Skill 18.1 Features of plants

The **non-vascular plants** represent a grade of evolution characterized by several primitive features for plants: lack of roots, lack of conducting tissues, rely on absorption of water that falls on the plant or they live in a zone of high humidity, and a lack of leaves or have microphylls (in ferns). Groups included are the liverworts, hornworts, and mosses. Each is recognized as a separate division.

The characteristics of **vascular plants** are as follows: synthesis of lignin to give rigidity and strength to cell walls for growing upright, evolution of tracheid cells for water transport and sieve cells for nutrient transport, and the use of underground stems (rhizomes) as a structure from which adventitious roots originate. There are two kinds of vascular plants: non-seeded and seeded. The non-seeded vascular plants divisions include Division Lycophyta – club moses, Division Sphenophyta – horsetails, and Division Pterophyta – ferns. The seeded vascular plants differ from the non-seeded plants by their method of reproduction, which will be discussed later.

The vascular seed plants are divided into two groups, the gymnosperms and the angiosperms. **Gymnosperms** were the first plants to evolve with the use of seeds for reproduction that made them less dependent on water to assist in reproduction. Their seeds and the pollen from the male are carried by the wind. Gymnosperms have cones that protect the seeds. Gymnosperm divisions include Division Cycadophyta – cycads, Division Ginkgophyta – ginkgo, Division Gnetophyta – gnetophytes, and Division Coniferophyta – conifers.

Angiosperms are the largest group in the plant kingdom. They are the flowering plants and produce true seeds for reproduction. They arose about seventy million years ago when the dinosaurs were disappearing. The land was drying up and the plants' ability to produce seeds that could remain dormant until conditions became acceptable allowed for their success. They also have more advanced vascular tissue and larger leaves for increased photosynthesis. Angiosperms consist of only one division, the Anthrophyta. Angiosperms are divided into monocots and dicots. Monocots have one cotelydon (seed leaf) and parallel veins on their leaves. Their flower petals are in multiples of threes. Dicots have two cotelydons and branching veins on their leaves. Flower petals are in multiples of fours or fives.

Skill 18.2 Reproduction and development of plants

Reproduction by plants is accomplished through alternation of generations. Simply stated, a haploid stage in the plants life history alternates with a diploid stage. The diploid sporophyte divides by meiosis to reduce the chromosome number to the haploid gametophyte generation. The haploid gametophytes undergo mitosis to produce gametes (sperm and eggs). Then, the haploid gametes fertilize to return to the diploid sporophyte stage.

The non-vascular plants need water to reproduce. The vascular non-seeded plants reproduce with spores and also need water to reproduce. Gymnosperms use seeds for reproduction and do not require water.

Angiosperms are the most numerous and are therefore the main focus of reproduction in this section. The sporophyte is the dominant phase in reproduction. Angiosperm reproductive structures are the flowers.

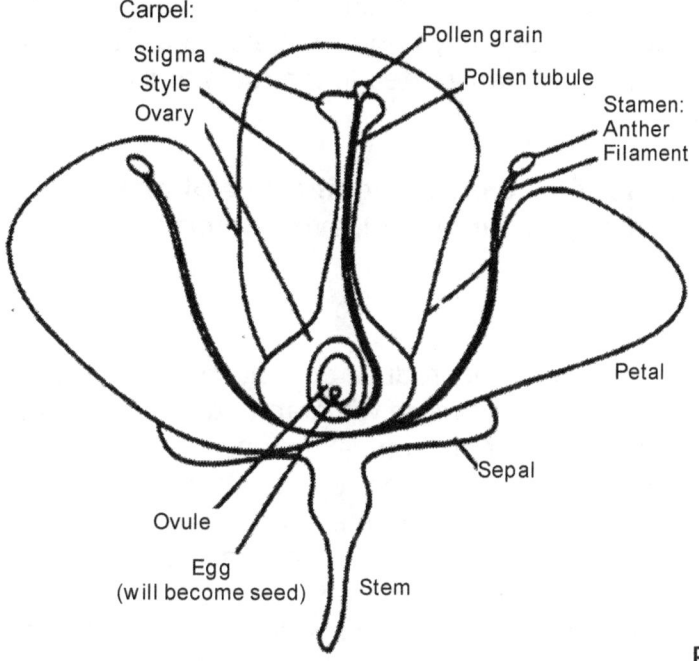

Figure 15

The male gametophytes are pollen grains and the female gametophytes are embryo sacs that are inside of the ovules. The male pollen grains are formed in the anthers at the tips of the stamens. The female ovules are enclosed by the ovaries. Therefore, the stamen is the reproductive organ of the male and the carpel is the reproductive organ of the female.

In a process called **pollination**, the pollen grains are released from the anthers and carried by animals and the wind and land on the carpels. The sperm is released to fertilize the eggs. Angiosperms reproduce through a method of double fertilization. An ovum is fertilized by two sperm. One sperm produces the new plant and the other forms the food supply for the developing plant (endosperm). The ovule develops into a seed and the ovary develops into a fruit. The fruit is then carried by wind or animals and the seeds are dispersed to form new plants.

The development of the egg to form a plant occurs in three stages: growth; morphogenesis, the development of form, and cellular differentiation, the acquisition of a cell's specific structure and function.

Skill 18.3 Knowledge of transport in plants

Roots absorb water and minerals and exchange gases in the soil. The xylem transports water and minerals, called xylem sap, upwards. This is pulled upwards in a process called **transpiration**. Transpiration is the evaporation of water from leaves. Gases are exchanged through the leaves and photosynthesis occurs. The sugar produced by photosynthesis goes down the phloem in the phloem sap. This sap is transported to the roots and other non-photosynthetic parts of the plant.

Skill 18.4 Evaluate the adaptive significance of plant structures (e.g., sporangia, microphylls, modified leaves, colorful flowers).

Sporangia

Sporangia are structures that produce or contain spores. Spores are an adaptive mechanism. First, they are able to withstand harsh conditions. Second, spores allow the plant to alternate between sexual and asexual reproduction. This is called alternation of generations and represents a "compromise" that allows a species to reap the benefits of both methods of reproduction. They are found on angiosperms, gymnosperms, ferns, and mosses. The sporangia protect the spores as they are forming and until they are ready to be disseminated. Once the spores are mature, the sporangia break open and release the spores with a spring-like action. This allows them to be carried far by the wind or a passing animal. Sporangia include both microsporangia and megasporangia. Microsporangia are found on the stamens of flowers and on the microsporophylls of male conifer cones. Megasporangia are found on the carpels of flowers.

Microphylls

Microphylls are the leaves on plants in the division Lycopodiophyta, including quillworts and clubmosses. Microphylls are a type of leaf with a single, unbranched vein. The vascular structure ("vein") in a microphyll is of the simplest type, a protostele. This protostele delivers water and nutrients to the photosynthesizing tissue in the leaf, allowing it to grow larger than a non-vascularized leaf could. Indeed, microphylls grow very large in quillworts and were over a meter long in certain extinct species. The single, simple vascular structure in microphylls distinguishes them from megaphylls, which have branching veins and are found on most vascular plants. It is believed that microphylls and megaphylls evolved separately, even though they structures and evolutionary advantages are similar.

Leaf modifications

The function of leaves is to manufacture food. Leaves are sometimes modified to do other jobs. Depending on the necessity, leaves are modified for the survival of plants. There are generally 9 types of leaf modifications:

1. **Scale like** - leaf shaped like a scale or awn (juniper & Cedar)
2. **Needle** - long, slender, tubular or triangular leaf (Non flowering plants like Pine, Fir etc.)
3. **Bract like** - a modified, often reduced leaf holding a flower or a cluster of flowers, usually colored (Poinsettia)
4. **Cataphyll** - a reduced leaf usually modified for protection, such as bud scales and rhizome scales. Its main function is to protect the bud (Pear)
5. **Storage** - leaves are modified for the purpose of storing food (Onion, Garlic, Tulip, Lily)
6. **Succulent** - thick, fleshy leaf, usually modified for water storage found in areas of low rain fall (Crassula, Portulaca, Aloe vera, sedum)
7. **Tendril** - slender, twining, modified leaf or stem used for clinging to objects for support (Grape, Cucumber)
8. **Spine** - a leaf or leaf part modified into a sharp point (Cactus, Holly)
9. **Trichome or hair** - hair like outgrowths of epidermal cells of leaves (Geranium, Tomato, Chrysanthemum, Peach, Fuzz)

Flowers: Flowers are reproductive organs in plants.

The functions of flowers are two fold –
1. The brightly colored corolla or petals attract agents of pollination such as insects and birds

The corolla encloses and protects the stamens and pistil.

Competency 0019

Understand the characteristics, functions, and adaptations of animals.

Skill 19.1 Identify the general characteristics of vertebrate and invertebrate development

Animal tissue becomes specialized during development. The ectoderm (outer layer) becomes the epidermis or skin. The mesoderm (middle layer) becomes muscles and other organs beside the gut. The endoderm (inner layer) becomes the gut, also called the archenteron.

Sponges are the simplest animals and lack true tissue. They exhibit no symmetry.
Diploblastic animals have only two germ layers: the ectoderm and endoderm. They have no true digestive system. Diploblastic animals include the Cnideria (jellyfish). They exhibit radial symmetry.

Triploblastic animals have all three germ layers. Triploblastic animals can be further divided into:

> **Acoelomates** - have no defined body cavity. An example is the flatworm (Platyhelminthe), which must absorb food from a host's digestive system.
> **Pseudocoelomates** - have a body cavity but it is not lined by tissue from the mesoderm. An example is the roundworm (Nematoda).
> **Coelomates** - have a true fluid filled body cavity called a coelom derived from the mesoderm. Coelomates can further be divided into **protostomes** and **deuterostomes**. In the development of protostomes, the first opening becomes the mouth and the second opening becomes the anus. The mesoderm splits to form the coelom. In the development of deuterostomes, the mouth develops from the second opening and the anus from the first opening. The mesoderm hollows out to become the coelom. Protostomes include animals in phylums Mollusca, Annelida and Arthropoda. Deuterostomes include animals in phylums Ehinodermata and Vertebrata.

Development is defined as a change in form. Animals go through several stages of development after fertilization of the egg cell:

Cleavage - the first divisions of the fertilized egg. Cleavage continues until the egg becomes a blastula.
Blastula - the blastula is a hollow ball of undifferentiated cells.
Gastrulation - this is the time of tissue differentiation into the separate germ layers, the endoderm, mesoderm and ectoderm.
Neuralation - development of the nervous system.
Organogenesis - the development of the various organs of the body.

BIOLOGICAL SCIENCES

Skill 19.2 Knowledge of physiological processes of animals

Animals constantly require oxygen for cellular respiration and need to remove carbon dioxide from their bodies. The respiratory surface must be large and moist. Different animal groups have different types of respiratory organs to perform gas exchange. Some animals use their entire outer skin for respiration (as in the case of worms).

Fishes and other aquatic animals have gills for gas exchange. Ventilation increases the flow of water over the gills. This process brings oxygen and removes carbon dioxide through the gills. Fish use a large amount of energy to ventilate its gills. This is because the oxygen available in water is less than that available in the air. The arthropoda (insects) have tracheal tubes that send air to all parts of their bodies.

Gas exchange for smaller insects is provided by diffusion. Larger insects ventilate their bodies by a series of body movements that compress and expand the tracheal tubes.

Vertebrates have lungs as their primary respiratory organ. The gas exchange system in all vertebrates is similar to that in humans discussed in a later section.

Osmoregulation and excretion in many invertebrates involves tubular systems. The tubules branch throughout the body. Interstitial fluid enters these tubes and is collected into excretory ducts that empty into the external environment by openings in the body wall. Insects have excretory organs called Malpighian tubes. These organs pump water, salts, and nitrogenous waste into the tubules. These fluids then pass through the hindgut and out the rectum. Vertebrates have kidneys as the primary excretion organ. This system is described in a later section.

Skill 19.3 Predict relative metabolic rates of animals (e.g., endotherms, ectotherms, animals of different sizes).

Several factors affect the metabolic rate of animals. However, certain trends do emerge. Remember that here we are discussing only resting or basal metabolism. Active metabolisms of all animals are frequently many times higher than their basal metabolic rates.

Endothermic (warm-blooded) organisms typically have faster metabolisms than ectothermic (cold-blooded) animals. Ectothermic species are usually bradymetabolic, meaning they have slow basal metabolisms. Bradymetabolic animals typically undergo large changes in metabolic rate, as available food and temperature dictates. This can be energetically favorable, since it allows these species to enter states of extremely low metabolism when conditions are unfavorable. Endothermic species, on the other hand, are typically tachymetabolic. These organisms must maintain a higher rate of metabolism at all times to sustain their internal environment. Again there are large differences between their basal and active metabolic rates, but these differences are not as extreme as in bradymetabolic species. While these tachymetabolic species cannot deal with food shortages by "shutting down" as bradymetabolic species do, they do have certain advantages. Specifically, they can maintain an environment optimal for the various biochemical reactions that sustain life.

Additionally, in both endotherms and ectotherms, metabolic rate is generally inversely related to body size. That is, smaller animals have higher metabolic rates per gram of body tissue. It is easy to understand why this is the case in endothermic animals; smaller animals have a greater surface to volume ratio and so lose heat at a faster rate. Therefore, these smaller animals must metabolize their food faster to compensate for this more rapid heat loss. Why this relationship between size and metabolic rate exists in ectotherms is a bit more complicated since cold blooded animals do not respond to heat loss by increasing their metabolism. In fact, the cause of this relationship in ectotherms is still not entirely understood. Some believe it is a result of the larger skeletal systems possessed by bigger animals. Since this skeletal tissue is fairly inactive metabolically, the overall metabolic rate for the animal is lower.

Skill 19.4 Analyze the importance of animal behaviors

Animal behavior is responsible for courtship leading to mating, communication between species, territoriality, and aggression between animals and dominance within a group. Behaviors may include body posture, mating calls, display of feathers or fur, coloration or bearing of teeth and claws.

Innate behaviors are inborn or instinctual. An environmental stimulus such as the length of day or temperature results in a behavior. Hibernation among some animals is an innate behavior. **Learned behavior** is modified due to past experience.

Competency 0020

Understand the structures and functions of the human skeletal, muscular, and integumentary systems; common malfunctions of these systems; and their homeostatic relationships within the body.

Skill 20.1 Structures, locations, and functions of the three types of muscular tissue

The muscular system's function is for movement. There are three types of muscle tissue. **Skeletal muscle** is voluntary. These muscles are attached to bones and are responsible for their movement. Skeletal muscle consists of long fibers and is striated due to the repeating patterns of the myofilaments (made of the proteins actin and myosin) that make up the fibers.

Cardiac muscle is found in the heart. Cardiac muscle is striated like skeletal muscle, but differs in that plasma membrane of the cardiac muscle causes the muscle to beat even when away from the heart. The action potentials of cardiac and skeletal muscles also differ.

Smooth muscle is involuntary. It is found in organs and enable functions such as digestion and respiration. Unlike skeletal and cardiac muscle, smooth muscle is not striated. Smooth muscle has less myosin and does not generate as much tension as the striated muscles.

Skill 20.2 Understand the mechanism of skeletal muscle contraction

A nerve impulse strikes a muscle fiber. This causes calcium ions to flood the sarcomere. Calcium ions allow ATP to expend energy. The myosin fibers creep along the actin, causing the muscle to contract. Once the nerve impulse has passed, calcium is pumped out and the contraction ends.

Skill 20.3 Analyze the movement of body joints

The axial skeleton consists of the bones of the skull and vertebrae. The appendicular skeleton consists of the bones of the legs, arms and tail, and shoulder girdle. Bone is a connective tissue. Parts of the bone include compact bone which gives strength, spongy bone which contains red marrow to make blood cells, yellow marrow in the center of long bones to store fat cells, and the periosteum which is the protective covering on the outside of the bone.

A joint is defined as a place where two bones meet. Joints enable movement. Ligaments attach bone to bone. Tendons attach bone to muscle. Joints allow great flexibility in movement. There are three types of joints:

1. Ball and socket – allows for rotation movement. An example is the joint between the shoulder and the humerus. This joint allows humans to move their arms and legs in many different ways.
2. Hinge – movement is restricted to a single plane. An example is the joint between the humerus and the ulna.
3. Pivot – allows for the rotation of the forearm at the elbow and the hands at the wrist.

Skill 20.4 Knowledge of the structure and function of the skin

The skin consists of two distinct layers. The epidermis is the thinner outer layer and the dermis is the thicker inner layer. Layers of tightly packed epithelial cells make up the epidermis. The tight packaging of the epithelial cells supports the skin's function as a protective barrier against infection.

The top layer of the epidermis consists of dead skin cells and is filled with keratin, a waterproofing protein. The dermis layer consists of connective tissue. It contains blood vessels, hair follicles, sweat glands, and sebaceous glands. An oily secretion called sebum, produced by the sebaceous gland, is released to the outer epidermis through the hair follicles. Sebum maintains the pH of the skin between 3 and 5, which inhibits most microorganism growth.

The skin also plays a role in thermoregulation. Increased body temperature causes skin blood vessels to dilate, resulting in heat radiating from the skin's surface. The sweat glands are also activated, increasing evaporative cooling. Decreased body temperature causes skin blood vessels to constrict. This results in blood from the skin diverting to deeper tissues and reduces heat loss from the surface of the skin.

Skill 20.5 Demonstrate an understanding of possible causes and effects of malfunctions of the skeletal, muscular, and integumentary systems (e.g., arthritis, skin cancer).

Here we consider five common malfuctions of the skeletal, muscular, and intdgumentary systems: arthritis, skin cancer, scoliosis, osteoporosis, and muscular dystrophy.

Arthritis is disease of the joints that causes pain and loss of movement. Inflammation, pain, and stiffness are the main symptoms of the various types of arthritis. Inflammation is the immune system's response to invasion by foreign bodies or damaged cells and tissue. The symptoms of inflammation (redness, swelling, etc.) result from increased blood flow and fluid leakage into the diseased area caused by chemicals released by immune cells.

Two of the most common types of arthritis are osteoarthritis and rheumatoid arthritis. The cause of osteoarthritis is the gradual breakdown of joint tissue associated with aging and prolonged "wear and tear". The underlying cause of rheumatoid arthritis is unknown. Rheumatoid arthritis is an autoimmune disease in which the body's immune system recognizes healthy tissue (usually joint tissue) as foreign and attacks it.

There is no known way to prevent rheumatoid arthritis, but weight management and avoiding joint injury and over use may prevent or delay the onset of osteoarthritis. The main treatments for arthritis are physical therapy and first and second-line drugs. Regular physical therapy helps maintain joint mobility and range of motion. First-line drugs, such as non-steroidal anti-inflammatory drugs (e.g. aspirin, ibuprofen, and naproxen), corticosteroids, and cox-2 inhibitors (e.g. Celebrex®), provide direct analgesic and anti-inflammatory relief. Second-line drugs used to treat rheumatoid arthritis, such as gold salts, sulfasalazine, methotrexate, chloroquine, hydroxychloroquine, and azathioprine, may delay the progression of the disease symptoms.

Skin cancer is the presence of malignant cells in the outer layers of the skin. The causes of skin cancer are sunburn, *uv* light damage, and heredity. Skin cancers are changes in the skin, such as growths, non-healing sores, or small lumps. Melanoma, the most dangerous type of skin cancer, can quickly spread to other parts of the body if left untreated. Limiting direct sun exposure and sunburns is the best means of preventing skin cancer. The first-line treatment for skin cancer is excision of the growth or malignancy.

Scoliosis is side-to-side curvature of the spine. The cause of scoliosis is unknown in most cases. Some serious types of scoliosis are caused by spinal birth defects, muscular or nerve damage, and deterioration of bone between the vertebrae. Most minor cases of scoliosis require little more than careful observation while more serious cases may require bracing or surgery. There is no known way to prevent scoliosis, but bracing can prevent progression of the disease.

Osteoporosis is the loss of bone mass leading to brittle bones, neck and back, pain, loss of height, and rounded shoulders. Some causes of osteoporosis are aging, sedentary lifestyle, smoking, calcium and vitamin D deficiency, decreased estrogen levels in women, and long-term use of corticosteroid drugs. Engaging in regular exercise, consuming a diet rich in calcium and vitamin D, refraining from smoking, and limiting caffeine and alcohol consumption may prevent osteoporosis. Hormone replacement treatment is the main treatment for osteoporosis. Other drugs used to treat osteoporosis include biphosphonates, raloxifene, alendronate, and calcitonin.

Muscular dystrophy is a disease characterized by a gradual decrease in muscle size and strength. Muscular dystrophy is caused by wasting of muscle tissue and is a genetic disease. There is no cure for muscular dystrophy and the goal of the main treatments – corticosteroids, physical therapy, and surgery – is management of complications. In addition, there is no way to prevent muscular dystrophy.

Competency 0021

Understand the structures and functions of the human respiratory and excretory systems, common malfunctions of these systems, and their homeostatic relationships within the body.

Skill 21.1 Surface area, volume, and function of the respiratory and excretory systems

The lungs are the respiratory surface of the human respiratory system. A dense net of capillaries contained just beneath the epithelium form the respiratory surface. The surface area of the epithelium is about 100m^2 in humans. Based on the surface area, the volume of air inhaled and exhaled is the tidal volume. This is normally about 500mL in adults. Vital capacity is the maximum volume the lungs can inhale and exhale. This is usually around 3400mL.

The kidneys are the primary organ in the excretory system. The pair of kidneys in humans are about 10cm long each. They receive about 20% of the blood pumped with each heartbeat despite their small size. The function of the excretory system is to rid the body of nitrogenous wastes in the form of urea.

Skill 21.2 Knowledge of process of breathing and gas exchange

The respiratory system functions in the gas exchange of oxygen and carbon dioxide waste. It delivers oxygen to the bloodstream and picks up carbon dioxide for release out of the body. Air enters the mouth and nose, where it is warmed, moistened and filtered of dust and particles. Cilia in the trachea trap unwanted material in mucus, which can be expelled. The trachea splits into two bronchial tubes and the bronchial tubes divide into smaller and smaller bronchioles in the lungs. The internal surface of the lung is composed of alveoli, which are thin walled air sacs. These allow for a large surface area for gas exchange. The alveoli are lined with capillaries. Oxygen diffuses into the bloodstream and carbon dioxide diffuses out of the capillaries to be exhaled out of the lungs due to partial pressure. The oxygenated blood is carried to the heart and delivered to all parts of the body by hemoglobin, a protein consisting of iron.

The thoracic cavity holds the lungs. The diaphragm muscle below the lungs is an adaptation that makes inhalation possible. As the volume of the thoracic cavity increases, the diaphragm muscle flattens out and inhalation occurs. When the diaphragm relaxes, exhalation occurs.

Skill 21.3 Knowledge of osmoregulation and waste removal

The functional unit of excretion is the nephron, which makes up the kidneys.

The structures of the excretory system and the nephron are as follows:

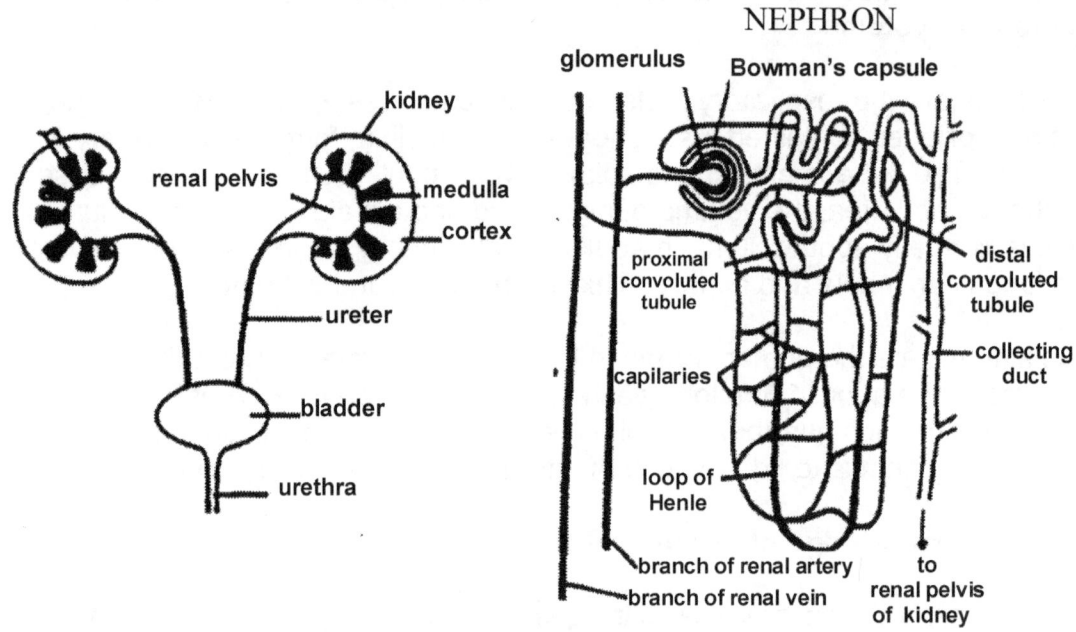

The Bowman's capsule contains the glomerulus, a tightly packed group of capillaries in the nephron. The glomerulus is under high pressure. Water, urea, salts, and other fluids leak out due to pressure into the Bowman's capsule. This fluid waste (filtrate) passes through the three regions of the nephron: the proximal convulated tubule, the loop of Henle, and the distal tubule. In the proximal convoluted tubule, unwanted molecules are secreted into the filtrate. In the loop of Henle, salt is actively pumped out of the tube and much water is lost due to the hyperosmosity of the inner part (medulla) of the kidney. As the fluid enters the distal tubule, more water is reabsorbed. Urine forms in the collecting duct that leads to the ureter then to the bladder where it is stored. Urine is passed from the bladder through the urethra. The amount of water reabsorbed back into the body is dependent upon how much water or fluids an individual has consumed. Urine can be very dilute or very concentrated if dehydration is present.

Skill 21.4 Malfunctions of the respiratory and excretory systems

Emphysema is a chronic obstructive pulmonary disease (COPD). These diseases make it difficult for a person to breathe. Airflow through the bronchial tubes is partially blocked making breathing difficult. The primary cause of emphysema is cigarette smoke. People with a deficiency in $alpha_1$-antitrypsin protein production have a greater risk of developing emphysema and at an earlier age. This protein helps protect the lungs from damage done by inflammation. This genetic deficiency is rare and can be tested for in individuals with a family history of the deficiency. There is no cure for emphysema but there are treatments available. The best prevention against emphysema is to not smoke.

Nephritis usually occurs in children. Symptoms include hypertension, decreased renal function, hematuria, and edema. Glomerulonephritis (GN) generally is a more precise term to describe this disease. Nephritis is produced by an antigen-antibody complex that causes inflammation and cell proliferation. Normal kidney tissue is damaged and if left untreated, nephritis can lead to kidney failure and death.

Competency 0022

Understand the structures and functions of the human circulatory and immune systems, common malfunctions of these systems, and their homeostatic relationships within the body.

Skill 22.1 Analyze the structure, function, and regulation of the heart

The function of the closed circulatory system (**cardiovascular system**) is to carry oxygenated blood and nutrients to all cells of the body and return carbon dioxide waste to be expelled from the lungs. The heart, blood vessels, and blood make up the cardiovascular system. The structure of the heart is shown below:

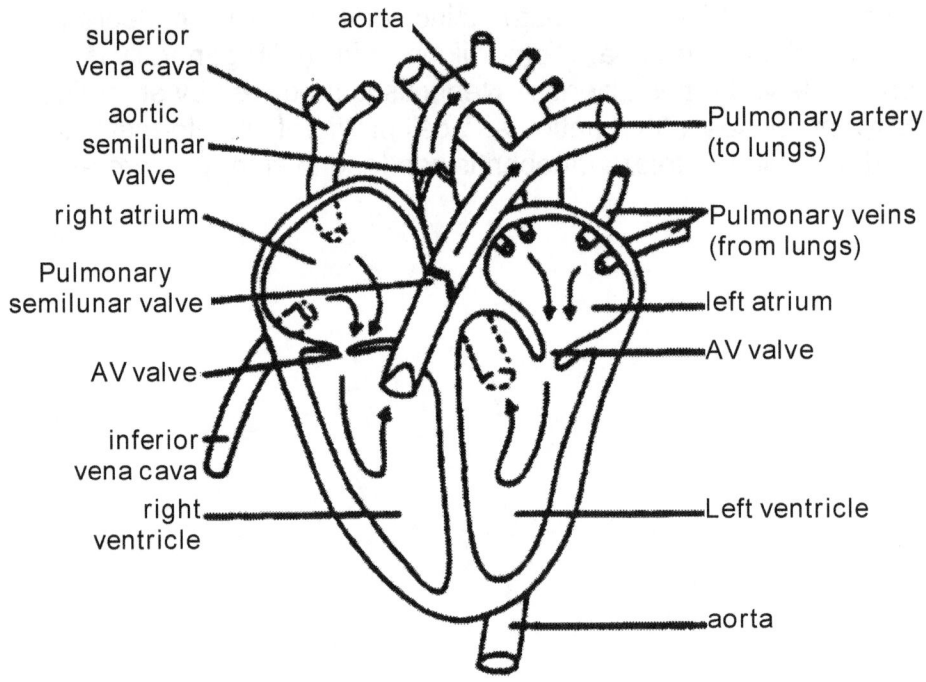

The atria are the chambers that receive blood returning to the heart and the ventricles are the chambers that pump blood out of the heart. There are four valves, two atrioventricular (AV) valves and two semilunar valves. The AV valves are located between each atrium and ventricle. The contraction of the ventricles closes the AV valve to keep blood from flowing back into the atria. The semilunar valves are located where the aorta leaves the left ventricle and the pulmonary artery leaves the right ventricle. The semilunar valves are opened by ventricular contraction to allow blood to be pumped out into the arteries and closed by the relaxation of the ventricles.

The cardiac output is the volume of blood per minute that the left ventricle pumps. This output depends on the heart rate and stroke volume. The **heart rate** is the number of times the heart beats per minute and the **stroke volume** is the amount of blood pumped by the left ventricle each time it contracts. Humans have an average cardiac output of about 5.25 L/min. Heavy exercise can increase cardiac output up to five times. Epinephrine and increased body temperature also increase heart rate and thus the cardiac output.

Cardiac muscle can contract without any signal from the nervous system. It is the sinoatrial node that is the pacemaker of the heart. It is located on the wall of the right atrium and generates electrical impulses that make the cardiac muscle cells contract in unison. The atrioventricular node shortly delays the electrical impulse to ensure the atria empty before the ventricles contract.

Skill 22.2 Malfunctions of the circulatory system

Cardiovascular diseases are the leading cause of death in the United States. Cardiac disease usually results in either a heart attack or a stroke. A heart attack is when cardiac muscle tissue dies, usually from coronary artery blockage. A stroke is when nervous tissue in the brain dies due to the blockage of arteries in the head.

Many heart attacks and strokes are caused by a disease called atherosclerosis. Plaques form on the inner walls of arteries, narrowing the area in which blood can flow. Arteriosclerosis is when the arteries harden from the plaque accumulation. Atherosclerosis can be prevented by a healthy diet limiting the lipids and cholesterol and exercise. High blood pressure (hypertension) promotes atherosclerosis. Diet, medication, and exercise can reduce high blood pressure and prevent atherosclerosis.

Skill 22.3 Structure, function, and regulation of the immune system

The immune system is responsible for defending the body against foreign invaders. There are two defense mechanisms: non specific and specific.

The **non-specific** immune mechanism has two lines of defenses. The first line of defense is the physical barriers of the body. These include the skin and mucous membranes. The skin prevents the penetration of bacteria and viruses as long as there are no abrasions on the skin. Mucous membranes form a protective barrier around the digestive, respiratory, and genitourinary tracts. Also, the pH of the skin and mucous membranes inhibit the growth of many microbes. Mucous secretions (tears and saliva) wash away many microbes and contain lysozyme that kills many microbes.

The second line of defense includes white blood cells and the inflammatory response. **Phagocytosis** is the ingestion of foreign particles. Neutrophils make up about seventy percent of all white blood cells. Monocytes mature to become macrophages which are the largest phagocytic cells. Eosinophils are also phagocytic. Natural killer cells destroy the body's own infected cells instead of the invading the microbe directly.

The other second line of defense is the inflammatory response. The blood supply to the injured area is increased, causing redness and heat. Swelling also typically occurs with inflammation. Histamine is released by basophils and mast cells when the cells are injured. This triggers the inflammatory response.

The **specific** immune mechanism recognizes specific foreign material and responds by destroying the invader. These mechanisms are specific and diverse. They are able to recognize individual pathogens. An **antigen** is any foreign particle that elicits an immune response. An **antibody** is manufactured by the body and recognizes and latches onto antigens, hopefully destroying them. They also have recognition of foreign material versus the self. Memory of the invaders provides immunity upon further exposure.

Immunity is the body's ability to recognize and destroy an antigen before it causes harm. Active immunity develops after recovery from an infectious disease (i.e. chicken pox) or after a vaccination (mumps, measles, rubella). Passive immunity may be passed from one individual to another and is not permanent. A good example is the immunities passed from mother to nursing child. A baby's immune system is not well developed and the passive immunity they receive through nursing keeps them healthier.

There are two main responses made by the body after exposure to an antigen:

1. **Humoral response** - free antigens activate this response and B cells (a lymphocyte from bone marrow) give rise to plasma cells that secrete antibodies and memory cells that will recognize future exposures to the same antigen. The antibodies defend against extracellular pathogens by binding to the antigen and making them an easy target for phagocytes to engulf and destroy. Antibodies are in a class of proteins called immunoglobulins. There are five major classes of immunoglobulins (Ig) involved in the humoral response: IgM, IgG, IgA, IgD, and IgE.

2. **Cell mediated response** - cells that have been infected activate T cells (a lymphocyte from the thymus). These activated T cells defend against pathogens in the cells or cancer cells by binding to the infected cell and destroying them along with the antigen. T cell receptors on the T helper cells recognize antigens bound to the body's own cells. T helper cells release IL-2 which stimulates other lymphocytes (cytotoxic T cells and B cells). Cytotoxic T cells kill infected host cells by recognizing specific antigens.

Vaccines are antigens given in very small amounts. They stimulate both humoral and cell mediated responses and memory cells recognize future exposure to the antigen so antibodies can be produced much faster.

Skill 22.4 Malfunctions of the immune system

The immune system attacks not only microbes but cells that are not native of the host. This is the problem with skin grafts, organ transplantations, and blood transfusions. Antibodies to foreign blood and tissue types already exist in the body. If blood is transfused that is not compatible with the host, these antibodies destroy the new blood cells. There is a similar reaction when tissue and organs are transplanted.

The major histocompatibility complex (MHC) is responsible for the rejection of tissue and organ transplants. This complex is unique to each person. Cytotoxic T cells recognize the MHC on the transplanted tissue or organ as foreign and destroy these tissues. Various drugs are needed to suppress the immune system so this does not happen. The complication with this is that the patient is now more susceptible to infection.

Autoimmune disease occurs when the body's own immune system destroys its own cells. Lupus, Grave's disease, and rheumatoid arthritis are examples of autoimmune disease. There is no way to prevent autoimmune diseases. Immunodeficiency is a deficiency in either the humoral or cell mediated immune defenses. HIV is an example of an immunodeficiency disease.

Competency 0023

Understand human nutrition and the structures and functions of the human digestive system and accessory organs, common malfunctions of the digestive system, and its homeostatic relationships within the body.

Skill 23.1 Understand the roles of basic nutrients found in foods

The function of the digestive system is to break food down into nutrients and absorb it into the blood stream where it can be delivered to all cells of the body for use in cellular respiration.

Essential nutrients are those nutrients that the body needs but cannot make. There are four groups of essential nutrients: essential amino acids, essential fatty acids, vitamins, and minerals.

There are about eight essential amino acids humans need. A lack of these amino acids results in protein deficiency. There are only a few essential fatty acids.

Vitamins are organic molecules essential for a nutritionally adequate diet. Thirteen vitamins essential to humans have been identified. There are two groups of vitamins: water soluble (includes the vitamin B complex and vitamin C) and water insoluble (vitamins A, D and K). Vitamin deficiencies can cause severe problems.

Unlike vitamins, minerals are inorganic molecules. Calcium is needed for bone construction and maintenance. Iron is important in cellular respiration and is a big component of hemoglobin.

Carbohydrates, fats, and proteins are fuel for the generation of ATP. Water is necessary to keep the body hydrated. The importance of water was discussed in previous sections.

Skill 23.2 Understand mechanical and chemical digestion

The teeth and saliva begin digestion by breaking food down into smaller pieces and lubricating it so it can be swallowed. The lips, cheeks, and tongue form a bolus or ball of food. It is carried down the pharynx by the process of peristalsis (wave-like contractions) and enters the stomach through the sphincter, which closes to keep food from going back up. In the stomach, pepsinogen and hydrochloric acid form pepsin, the enzyme that hydrolyzes proteins. The food is broken down further by this chemical action and is churned into acid chyme. The pyloric sphincter muscle opens to allow the food to enter the small intestine. Most nutrient absorption occurs in the small intestine. Its large surface area, accomplished by its length and protrusions called villi and microvilli, allow for a great absorptive surface into the bloodstream. Chyme is neutralized after coming from the acidic stomach to allow the enzymes found there to function.

Accessory organs function in the production of necessary enzymes and bile. The pancreas makes many enzymes to break down food in the small intestine. The liver makes bile, which breaks down and emulsifies fatty acids. Any food left after the trip through the small intestine enters the large intestine. The large intestine functions to reabsorb water and produce vitamin K. The feces, or remaining waste, are passed out through the anus.

Skill 23.3 Malfunctions of the digestive system

Gastric ulcers are lesions in the stomach lining. Ulcers are mainly caused by bacteria, but are worsened by pepsin and acid if the ulcers are not healed quickly enough.

Appendicitis is the inflammation of the appendix. The appendix has no known function but is open to the intestine, but can be blocked by hardened stool or swollen tissue. The blocked appendix can cause bacterial infections and inflammation leading to appendicitis. The swelling cuts the blood supply, killing the organ tissue. If left untreated, this leads to the rupture of the appendix and the stool and the infection spill out into the abdomen. This condition is life threatening if immediate surgery does not take place. Symptoms include lower abdominal pain, nausea, loss of appetite, and fever.

Anorexia, bulimia, and binge eating disorders are disorders of the digestive system. They include emotions, attitudes, and behaviors all relating to weight and food issues, and are typically caused by poor self-image and a unrealistic view of self. Anorexia Nervosa is a serious, life-threatening disorder. An anorexic person harms his/her body by self-starvation and excessive weight loss. Bulimia Nervosa is also a serious, potentially life-threatening eating disorder. In this disorder, participants binge and compensate for binges by means such as self-induced vomiting or laxative use. In the United States, as many as 10 million females and 1 million males are fighting a life and death battle with an eating disorder such as anorexia or bulimia. Approximately 25 million more are struggling with binge eating disorder (Crowther et al., 1992; Fairburn et al., 1993; Gordon, 1990; Hoek, 1995; Shisslak et al., 1995).

Competency 0024

Understand the structures and functions of the human nervous and endocrine systems, common malfunctions of these systems, and their homeostatic relationships within the body.

Skill 24.1 Knowledge of the central and peripheral nervous systems

The **central nervous system (CNS)** consists of the brain and spinal cord. The CNS is responsible for the body's response to environmental stimulation. The spinal cord is located inside the spine. It sends out motor commands for movement in response to stimuli. The brain is where responses to more complex stimuli occurs. The meninges are the connective tissues that protect the CNS. The CNS contains fluid filled spaces called ventricles. These ventricles are filled when cerebrospinal fluid which is formed in the brain. This fluid cushions the brain and circulates nutrients, white blood cells, and hormones. The CNS's response to stimuli is a reflex. The reflex is an unconscious, automatic response.

The **peripheral nervous system (PNS)** consists of the nerves that connect the CNS to the rest of the body. The sensory division brings information to the CNS from sensory receptors and the motor division sends signals from the CNS to effector cells. The motor division consists of somatic nervous system and the autonomic nervous system. The somatic nervous system is controlled consciously in response to external stimuli. The autonomic nervous system is unconsciously controlled by the hypothalamus of the brain to regulate the internal environment. This system is responsible for the movement of smooth and cardiac muscles as well as the muscles for other organ systems.

Skill 24.2 Analyze the role of nerve impulses and neurons

The **neuron** is the basic unit of the nervous system. It consists of an axon, which carries impulses away from the cell body to the tip of the neuron; the dendrite, which carries impulses toward the cell body; and the cell body, which contains the nucleus. Synapses are spaces between neurons. Chemicals called neurotransmitters are found close to the synapse. The myelin sheath, composed of Schwann cells cover the neurons and provide insulation.

Nerve action depends on depolarization and an imbalance of electrical charges across the neuron. A polarized nerve has a positive charge outside the neuron. A depolarized nerve has a negative charge outside the neuron. Neurotransmitters turn off the sodium pump that results in depolarization of the membrane. This wave of depolarization (as it moves from neuron to neuron) carries an electrical impulse. This is actually a wave of opening and closing gates that allows for the flow of ions across the synapse. Nerves have an action potential.

There is a threshold of the level of chemicals that must be met or exceeded in order for muscles to respond. This is called the "all or none" response.

Skill 24.3 Discuss the influence of drugs and other chemicals on nerve transmission

The drugs which affect our nervous system are mainly divided into three categories:

1. Stimulants: A stimulant is a drug that speeds up body activities that are controlled by the nervous system. Many stimulants are controlled drugs. Examples are cocaine and amphitamine. Caffeine and nicotine are also stimulants, but they are not controlled drugs.
How does a stimulant speed up body's activities? Neurons carry messages to the brain. Chemical messengers given off by the axon end of one neuron move across the synapse and are picked up by the dendrite end of the next neuron. Usually these chemical messengers are destroyed after crossing the synapse to prevent the original message from going on continuously.

The stimulants may cause the axon of the neuron to give off more of the chemical messenger than the normal or the stimulants may prevent the chemical messenger from being destroyed once it reaches the dendrite of the next neuron. In both cases the second neuron keeps receiving chemical messengers. With stimulants messages move from one neuron to the next for a longer time.

2. Depressants: A depressant slows down messages in the nervous system. They act exactly opposite to stimulants. Their main role is calm behavior. Depressants are controlled drugs. Examples are - mild sleep aids, morphine and barbiturates.

3. Psychedelic drugs: These alter the way the mind works and change the signals we receive from our sense organs. Hearing, seeing and thinking are changed. Senses blend together. Some one may report "tasting colors" and "seeing music". PCP and LSD are examples of psychedelic drugs. Natural psychedelic drugs are those found in certain kinds of mushrooms, cactus plants, marijuana, and the leaves of some desert and jungle plants.
Use of PCP causes physical changes including high blood pressure, difficulties with walking, standing and numbness. Users of PCP may become violent as well.

Inhalants are related to psychedelic drugs. Inhalants are drugs that are breathed through the lungs in order to cause a behavior change. The chemicals in glues, paints and correction fluids are inhalants. Their use can cause irregular heart beat, liver damage and in some cases, the heart may stop beating resulting in death.

Skill 24.4 Understand the feedback mechanisms in homeostasis

The thyroid gland produces hormones that help maintain heart rate, blood pressure, muscle tone, digestion, and reproductive functions. The parathyroid glands maintain the calcium level in blood and the pancreas maintains glucose homeostasis by secreting insulin and glucagon when necessary. The three gonadal steroids, androgen (testosterone), estrogen, and progesterone, regulate the development of the male and female reproductive organs.

Neurotransmitters are chemical messengers. The most common of which is acetylcholine. Acetylcholine controls muscle contraction and heartbeat. A group of neurotransmitters, the catecholamines, includes epinephrine and norepinephrine. Epinephrine (adrenaline) and norepinephrine are also hormones. They are produced in response to stress. They have profound effects on the cardiovascular and respiratory systems. These hormones/neurotransmitters can be used to increase the rate and stroke volume of the heart, thus increasing the rate of oxygen to the blood cells.

Skill 24.5 Malfunctions of the nervous and endocrine systems

Diabetes is the best known endocrine disorder. This is caused by a deficiency of insulin resulting in high blood glucose. Type I diabetes is an autoimmune disorder. The immune system attacks the cells of the pancreas, ending the ability to produce insulin. Treatment for type I diabetes consists of daily insulin injections. Type II diabetes usually occurs with age and/or obesity. There is usually a reduced response in target cells due to changes in insulin receptors or a deficiency of insulin. Type II diabetics need to monitor their blood glucose levels. Treatment is usually by diet and exercise.

Hyperthyroidism is another disorder of the endocrine system. This occurs from excessive secretion of thyroid hormones. Symptoms are weight loss, high blood pressure, and high body temperature. The opposite, hypothyroidism, causes weight gain, lethargy, and intolerance to cold.

There are many nervous system disorders. Parkinson's disease is caused by the degeneration of the basal ganglia in the brain. This results in the motor impulses send to the muscles to cease. Symptoms include tremors, slow movement, and muscle rigidity. Progression of Parkinson's disease occurs in five stages: early, mild, moderate, advanced, and severe. In the severe stage, the person is confined to a bed or chair. There is no cure for Parkinson's disease. Private research with stem cells is currently underway to find a cure for Parkinson's disease.

Competency 0025

Understand the structures and functions of the human reproductive systems, their homeostatic relationships within the body, processes of embryonic development, common malfunctions of the reproductive systems, and sexually transmitted diseases.

Skill 25.1 Understand the major endocrine glands and the function of their hormones

The function of the **endocrine system** is to manufacture proteins called hormones. **Hormones** are released into the bloodstream and are carried to a target tissue where they stimulate an action. There are two classes of hormones. Steroid hormones come from cholesterol and include the sex hormones. Peptide hormones are derived from amino acids. Hormones are specific and fit receptors on the target tissue cell surface. The receptor activates an enzyme that converts ATP to cyclic AMP. Cyclic AMP (cAMP) is a second messenger from the cell membrane to the nucleus. The genes found in the nucleus turn on or off to cause a specific response.

Hormones are secreted by endocrine cells which make up endocrine glands. The major endocrine glands and their hormones are as follows:

Hypothalamus – located in the lower brain; signals the pituitary gland.
Pituitary gland – located at the base of the hypothalamus; releases growth hormones and antidiuretic hormone (retention of water in kidneys).
Thyroid gland – located on the trachea; lowers blood calcium levels (calcitonin) and maintains metabolic processes (thyroxine).
Gonads – located in the testes of the male and the ovaries of the female; testes release androgens to support sperm formation and ovaries release estrogens to stimulate uterine lining growth and progesterone to promote uterine lining growth.
Pancreas – secretes insulin to lower blood glucose levels and glucagon to raise blood glucose levels.

Skill 25.2 Understand hormone control and development and function of male and female reproductive systems

Hormones regulate sexual maturation in humans. Humans cannot reproduce until about the puberty age of 8-14, depending on the individual. The hypothalamus begins secreting hormones that help mature the reproductive system and development of the secondary sex characteristics. Reproductive maturity in girls occurs with her first menstruation and occurs in boys with the first ejaculation of viable sperm.

BIOLOGICAL SCIENCES

Hormones also regulate reproduction. In males, the primary sex hormones are the androgens, testosterone being the most important. The androgens are produced in the testes and are responsible for the primary and secondary sex characteristics of the male. Female hormone patterns are cyclic and complex. Most women have a reproductive cycle length of about 28 days. The menstrual cycle is specific to the changes in the uterus. The ovarian cycle results in ovulation and occurs in parallel with the menstrual cycle. This parallelism is regulated by hormones. Five hormones participate in this regulation, most notably estrogen and progesterone. Estrogen and progesterone play an important role in the signaling to the uterus and the development and maintenance of the endometruim. Estrogens are also responsible for the secondary sex characteristics of females.

Skill 25.3 Gametogenesis, fertilization, and birth control

Gametogenesis is the production of the sperm and egg cells. **Spermatogenesis** begins at puberty in the male. One spermatogonia, the diploid precursor of sperm, produces four sperm. The sperm mature in the seminiferous tubules located in the testes. **Oogenesis**, the production of egg cells (ova), is usually complete by the birth of a female. Egg cells are not released until menstruation begins at puberty. Meiosis forms one ovum with all the cytoplasm and three polar bodies that are reabsorbed by the body. The ovum are stored in the ovaries and released each month from puberty to menopause.

Sperm are stored in the seminiferous tubules in the testes where they mature. Mature sperm are found in the epididymis located on top of the testes. After ejaculation, the sperm travels up the **vas deferens** where they mix with semen made in the prostate and seminal vesicles and travel out the urethra.

Ovulation releases the egg into the fallopian tubes that are ciliated to move the egg along. Fertilization of the egg by the sperm normally occurs in the fallopian tube. If pregnancy does not occur, the egg passes through the uterus and is expelled through the vagina during menstruation. Levels of progesterone and estrogen stimulate menstruation and are affected by the implantation of a fertilized egg so menstruation will not occur.

There are many methods of contraception (birth control) that affect different stages of fertilization. Chemical contraception (birth control pills) prevents ovulation by synthetic estrogen and progesterone. Several barrier methods of contraception are available. Male and female condoms block semen from contacting the egg. Sterilization is another method of birth control. Tubil ligation in women prevents eggs from entering the uterus. A vasectomy in men involves the cutting of the vas deferens. This prevents the sperm from entering the urethra. The most effective method of birth control is abstinence. Worldwide programs have been established to promote abstinence especially amongst teenagers.

Skill 25.4 Embryonic and fetal development

If fertilization occurs, the zygote begins dividing about 24 hours later. The resulting cells from a blastocyst and implants in about two to three days in the uterus. Implantation promotes secretion of human chorionic gonadotrophin (HCG). This is what is detected in pregnancy tests. The HCG keeps the level of progesterone elevated to maintain the uterine lining in order to feed the developing embryo until the umbilical cord forms.

Organogenesis, the development of the body organs, occurs during the first trimester of fetal development. The heart begins to beat and all the major structures are present at this time. The fetus grows very rapidly during the second trimester of pregnancy. The fetus is about 30 cm long and is very active at this stage. During the third and last trimester, fetal activity may decrease as the fetus grows. Labor is initiated by oxytocin, which causes labor contractions and dilation of the cervix. Prolactin and oxytocin cause the production of milk.

Skill 25.5 Potential effects of drugs, alcohol, and nutrition on fetal development.

In this section we will look at some of the potential effects of drugs, alcohol, and nutrition on the process of embryonic and fetal development.

1. Drugs: Cocaine and similar drugs are very detrimental for growth of the fetus. Exposed fetuses often have intrauterine growth retardation, microcephaly, cerebral infarction, urogeniital anomalies, an increased risk of sudden infant death syndrome as well as neurological and other behavioral abnormalities. These pregnancies are at risk for premature labor, spontaneous abortion, increased perinatal mortality, and fetal death.
Drugs are thought to induce birth defects by disrupting the vasculature in the placenta, thereby inducing intrauterine hypoxia and malnutrition.

2. Alcohol: Ethanol is the causative agent of Fetal Alcohol Syndrome (FAS). FAS is seen in approximately 2 in 1000 live births, depending upon culture and socio-economic status.
Alcohol is able to permeate the placenta and enter fetal circulatory system, thereby causing developmental abnormalities. Ethanol impairs placental blood flow to the fetus by constricting blood vessels: inducing hypoxia and fetal malnutrition.
Alcohol can cause the following in the fetuses:
Growth deficiencies, micropthalmia, microcephaly, small brain size, cardiovascular disorders, besides a host of others.

3. Nutrition: Nutrition of the mother during pregnancy plays a vital role in the development of the fetus. Malnutrition can lead to a host of complications including brain growth and development.

Skill 25.6 Malfunctions of the reproductive systems (e.g., infertility, birth defects).

The most common diseases or disorders in relation to the reproductive system are infertility, endometriosis and cancer of the reproductive organs. Infertility is defined as not being able to get pregnant after at least one year of trying. Women who are able to get pregnant but then have repeat miscarriages are also said to be infertile.

Causes of infertility in men:
1. Problems making sperm or making a few sperms
2. Problems with the mobility of the sperm in reaching the egg
3. Men born with problems that affect the sperm

The following factors increase the risk of infertility in men: alcohol, drugs, smoking cigarettes environmental toxins - pesticides and lead, health problems, medicines, radiation treatment and chemotherapy for cancer, age etc.

Causes of infertility in women: ovulation, blocked fallopian tubes due to endometriosis, age, and stress.

To cure infertility, doctors use a variety of treatments:
1. Surgery to treat infertility to correct problems with a woman's ovaries, fallopian tubes, or uterus.
2. Intrauterine insemination (IUI): is also known as artificial insemination, in which the woman is inseminated with specially prepared sperm.
3. Assisted reproductive Technology (ART) describes several different methods used to help infertile couples. ART involves removing eggs from a woman, fertilizing them outside of and them placing them back into her uterus.
Endometriosis is a disorder causing painful menstruation in a woman. Endometriosis causes endometrial tissue (the tissue lining the uterus) to grow/implant elsewhere in the body, mainly in the abdominal cavity. Some women will take medication to help them cope with symptoms. Occasionally fertility is affected.

Cancers of the reproductive systems include ovarian cancer, uterine cancer, cervical cancer and prostate cancer. As a society, we have come a long way in our fight against cancer. Survival rates for these cancers are improving. The best way to protect against these cancers is frequent screening. Ovarian cancer has vague symptoms such as abdominal bloating and pelvic discomfort. The most common form of uterine cancer is endometrial cancer, which is a cancer of the inner lining of the uterus. The most common symptom of endometrial cancer is unexpected vaginal bleeding.

This cancer has high survival rates when treated early. Risk factors include being over age 50, obesity, high blood pressure, diabetes, and HRT (hormone replacement therapy) without progestin accompaniment. Cervical cancer affects the lining of the cervix, the area joining the uterus and vagina. Pap smears are recommended yearly to check for this slow growing cancer. In addition, a new vaccine has just been approved and is suggested for all 11-12 year old girls. Prostate cancer affects males only. Prostate cancer has no apparent symptoms in the early stage and only vague symptoms later. According to the Prostate cancer Foundation, prostate cancer is the most common non-skin cancer in America, affecting 1 in 6 men. The older you are, the more likely you are to be diagnosed with prostate cancer. Many therapies exist, from surveillance only, to radiation, to hormone therapies.

Congenital disorder is a broad and difficult category. It encompasses the following possibilities:
1. Birth defect: a structural malformation of a body part, recognizable at birth.
2. Congenital physical anomaly is a difference (abnormality) of the structure of a body part, which may or may not be recognized as a problem condition.
3. Congenital malformation is a problem affecting more than one body part.
4. Genetic disorders may not be apparent at the beginning but will be expressed later in life.
5. Congenital metabolic diseases are also known as inborn errors of metabolism. Most of these are single gene defects.
6. Sporadic birth defects are whose causes are not known. They are random and a low recurrence risk for future children.

Skill 25. 7 Demonstrate an understanding of sexually transmitted diseases.

Sexually transmitted diseases (STDs) include diseases and infections that have high probability of being transmitted between people via sexual contact. This sexual contact can include vaginal intercourse, oral sex, or anal sex. Accordingly, STDs are typically transmitted through the mucous membranes of the penis, vagina, mouth, and anus. Because mucous membranes support pathogens more easily than skin, the probability of disease transmission is higher for sexual than non-sexual contact. STDs may be bacterial, viral, or parasitic in nature. Common STDs include:

Bacterial: chlamydia, gonorrhea, and syphilis
Viral: hepatitis B, herpes, HIV/AIDS, human papillomavirus (HPV)
Parasitic: public lice, scabies

STDs can be transmitted whether or not a person exhibits symptoms of the disease. Public health campaigns in America now typically aim to control the spread of HIV/AIDS and place emphasis on the fact that all sexual activities carry a risk of STD transmission. Healthcare professionals advocate the practice of safe sex to greatly reduce the odds of contracting an STD, though abstinence is the only absolute safeguard. It should also be noted that other forms of bodily fluid exchange (needle sharing, blood transfusion, etc) can transmit STDs.

The treatment of STDs depends, of course, on the cause of the disease. Those of bacterial origin can usually be treated with a course of antibiotics. Anti-parasitic creams and shampoos are used to treat diseases of parasitic origin. Viral STDs are more difficult to treat. Currently, medications are available to slow replication of viruses and to treat the symptoms of these STDs. However, STDs of viral origin cannot be cured by modern medicine at present.

Competency 0026

Understand the characteristics of populations and communities, and use this knowledge to analyze population growth and community interactions.

Skill 26.1 Factors that affect population size and growth rate

A **population** is a group of individuals of one species that live in the same general area. Many factors can affect the population size and its growth rate. Population size can depend on the total amount of life a habitat can support. This is the carrying capacity of the environment. Once the habitat runs out of food, water, shelter, or space, the carrying capacity decreases, and then stabilizes.

Limiting factors can affect population growth. As a population increases, the competition for resources is more intense, and the growth rate declines. This is a **density-dependent** growth factor. The carrying capacity can be determined by the density-dependent factor. **Density-independent factors** affect the individuals regardless of population size. The weather and climate are good examples. Too hot or too cold temperatures may kill many individuals from a population that has not reached its carrying capacity.

Skill 26.2 Population growth curves

Zero population growth rate occurs when the birth and death rates are equal in a population. Exponential growth rate occurs when there is and abundance of resources and the growth rate is at its maximum, called the intrinsic rate of increase. This relationship can be understood in a growth curve.

An exponentially growing population starts off with a little change, then rapidly increases.

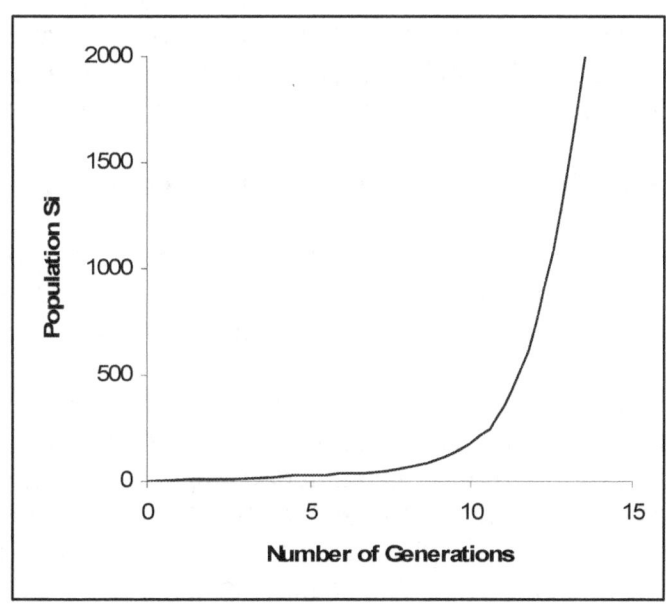

Logistic population growth incorporates the carrying capacity into the growth rate. As a population reaches the carrying capacity, the growth rate begins to slow down and level off.

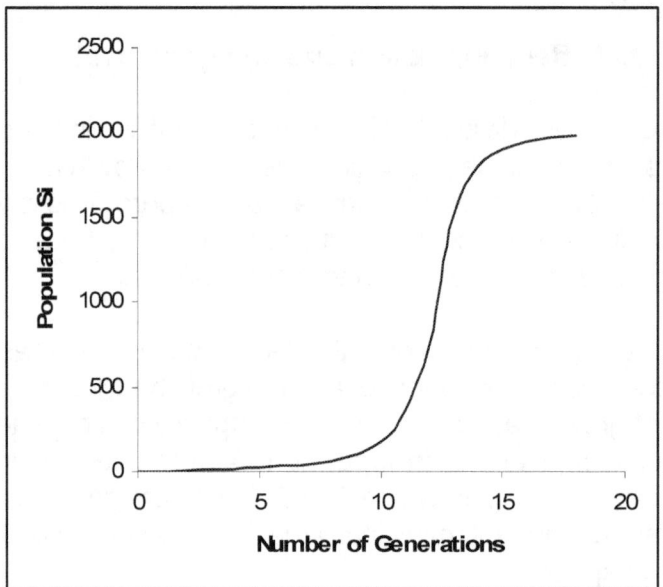

Many populations follow this model of population growth. Humans, however, are an exponentially growing population. Eventually, the carrying capacity of the Earth will be reached, and the growth rate will level off. How and when this will occur remains a mystery.

Logarithmic growth exists when size/abundance/occurrence can be described as a logarithm where $y = C \log(x)$. Logarithmic growth is very slow and is the inverse of exponential growth. Bacteria follow a logarithmic growth pattern. **Exponential growth** is characterized by back-to-back division cycles such that the population doubles in number every generation. For example, if at time 0 there were 10 cells present, then at time 200 there would exist 100 cells.

Skill 26.3 Relationships among organisms in a community

There are many interactions that may occur between different species living together. Predation, parasitism, competition, commensalisms, and mutualism are the different types of relationships populations have amongst each other.

Predation and **parasitism** result in a benefit for one species and a detriment for the other. Predation is when a predator eats its prey. The common conception of predation is of a carnivore consuming other animals. This is one form of predation. Although not always resulting in the death of the plant, herbivory is a form of predation. Some animals eat enough of a plant to cause death. Parasitism involves a predator that lives on or in their hosts, causing detrimental effects to the host.

Insects and viruses living off and reproducing in their hosts is an example of parasitism. Many plants and animals have defenses against predators. Some plants have poisonous chemicals that will harm the predator if ingested and some animals are camouflaged so they are harder to detect.

Competition is when two or more species in a community use the same resources. Competition is usually detrimental to both populations. Competition is often difficult to find in nature because competition between two populations is not continuous. Either the weaker population will no longer exist, or one population will evolve to utilize other available resources.

Symbiosis is when two species live close together. Parasitism is one example of symbiosis described above. Another example of symbiosis is commensalisms. **Commensalism** occurs when one species benefits from the other without harmful effects. **Mutualism** is when both species benefit from the other. Species involved in mutualistic relationships must coevolve to survive. As one species evolves, the other must as well if it is to be successful in life. The grouper and a species of shrimp live in a mutualistic relationship. The shrimp feed off parasites living on the grouper; thus the shrimp are fed and the grouper stays healthy. Many microorganisms are in mutualistic relationships.

Competency 0027

Understand the development and structure of ecosystems and the characteristics of major biomes.

Skill 27.1 Flow of energy through trophic levels of an ecosystem

Trophic levels are based on the feeding relationships that determine energy flow and chemical cycling.

Autotrophs are the primary producers of the ecosystem. **Producers** mainly consist of plants. **Primary consumers** are the next trophic level. The primary consumers are the herbivores that eat plants or algae. **Secondary consumers** are the carnivores that eat the primary consumers. **Tertiary consumers** eat the secondary consumer. These trophic levels may go higher depending on the ecosystem. **Decomposers** are consumers that feed off animal waste and dead organisms. This pathway of food transfer is known as the food chain.

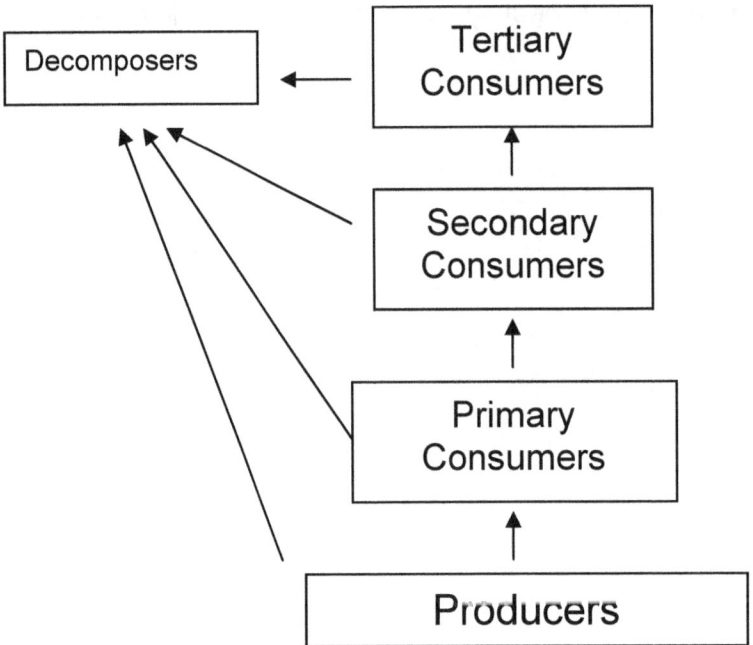

Most food chains are more elaborate, becoming food webs.

Skill 27.2 Pyramid models

Energy is lost as the trophic levels progress from producer to tertiary consumer. The amount of energy that is transferred between trophic levels is called the ecological efficiency. The visual of this energy flow is represented in a **pyramid of productivity**.

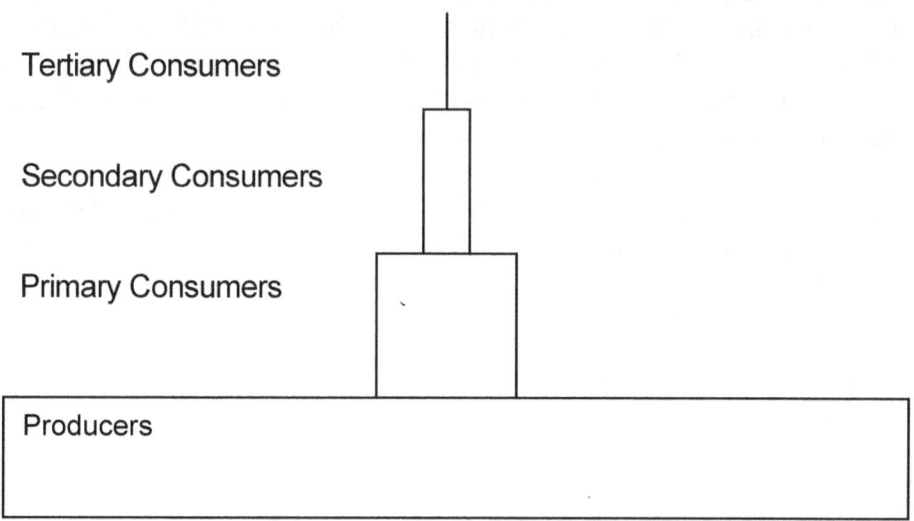

The **biomass pyramid** represents the total dry weight of organisms in each trophic level. A **pyramid of numbers** is a representation of the population size of each trophic level. The producers, being the most populous, are on the bottom of this pyramid with the tertiary consumers on the top with the fewest numbers.

Skill 27.3 Ecological succession and biotic and abiotic factors

Succession is an orderly process of replacing a community that has been damaged or has begun where no life previously existed. Primary succession occurs where life never existed before, as in a flooded area or a new volcanic island. Secondary succession takes place in communities that were once flourishing but disturbed by some source, either man or nature, but not totally stripped. A climax community is a community that is established and flourishing.

Abiotic and biotic factors play a role in succession. **Biotic factors** are living things in an ecosystem; plants, animals, bacteria, fungi, etc. **Abiotic factors** are non-living aspects of an ecosystem; soil quality, rainfall, temperature, etc.

Abiotic factors affect succession by way of the species that colonize the area. Certain species will or will not survive depending on the weather, climate, or soil makeup. Biotic factors such as inhibition of one species due to another may occur. This may be due to some form of competition between the species. **Biomes** are communities and ecosystems that are typical of broad geographic regions. Humans are continuously searching for new places to form communities. This encroachment on the environment leads to the destruction of wildlife communities. Conservationists focus on endangered species, but the primary focus should be on protecting the entire biome. If a biome becomes extinct, the wildlife dies or invades another biome.

Preservations established by the government aim at protecting small parts of biomes. While beneficial in the conservation of a few areas, the majority of the environment is still unprotected.

Competency 0028

Understand the connections within and among the biogeochemical cycles, and analyze their implications for living things.

Skill 28.1 Recognize the importance of the processes involved in the water cycle.

Water that falls to Earth in the form of rain and snow is called **precipitation.** Precipitation is part of a continuous process in which water at the Earth's surface evaporates, condenses into clouds, and returns to Earth. This process is termed the **water cycle**. Two percent of all the available water is fixed and unavailable in ice or the bodies of organisms. Available water includes surface water (lakes, ocean, rivers) and ground water (aquifers, wells). The water located below the surface is called groundwater. 96% of all available water is from ground water. The water cycle is driven by solar energy. Water is recycled. The water present now is the water that has been here since our atmosphere formed.

Altitude's impacts upon climatic conditions are primarily temperature and precipitation related. As altitude increases, climatic conditions become increasingly drier and colder. Solar radiation becomes more severe as altitude increases while the effects of convection forces are minimized. Climatic changes as a function of latitude follows a similar pattern (latitude moves either north or south from the equator). The climate becomes colder and drier as the distance from the equator increases. Proximity to land or water masses produces climatic conditions based upon the available moisture. Dry and arid climates prevail where moisture is scarce; lush tropical climates can prevail where moisture is abundant. Climate, as described above, depends upon the specific combination of conditions making up an area's environment. Man impacts all environments by producing pollutants in earth, air, and water. It follows then, that man is a major player in world climatic conditions.

Skill 28.2 Role of decomposers in nutrient cycling.

In the carbon cycle, decomposers recycle the carbon accumulated in durable organic material that do not immediately proceed to the carbon cycle. Ammonification is the decomposition of organic nitrogen back to ammonia. This process in the nitrogen cycle is carried out by aerobic and anaerobic bacterial and fungal decomposers. Decomposers add phosphorous back to the soil by decomposing the excretion of animals.

Skill 28.3 Analyze the role of respiration and photosynthesis in biogeochemical cycling.

Biogeochemical cycles are nutrient cycles that involve both biotic and abiotic factors.

Water cycle - 2% of all the available water is fixed and unavailable in ice or the bodies of organisms. Available water includes surface water (lakes, ocean, rivers) and ground water (aquifers, wells) 96% of all available water is from ground water. The water cycle is driven by solar energy. Water is recycled through the processes of evaporation and precipitation. The water present now is the water that has been here since our atmosphere formed.

Carbon cycle - Ten percent of all available carbon in the air (from carbon dioxide gas) is fixed by photosynthesis. Plants fix carbon in the form of glucose, animals eat the plants and are able to obtain their source of carbon. When animals release carbon dioxide through respiration, the plants again have a source of carbon to fix again.

Nitrogen cycle - Eighty percent of the atmosphere is in the form of nitrogen gas. Nitrogen must be fixed and taken out of the gaseous form to be incorporated into an organism. Only a few genera of bacteria have the correct enzymes to break the triple bond between nitrogen atoms in a process called nitrogen fixation. These bacteria live within the roots of legumes (peas, beans, alfalfa) and add nitrogen to the soil so it may be taken up by the plant. Nitrogen is necessary to make amino acids and the nitrogenous bases of DNA.

Phosphorus cycle - Phosphorus exists as a mineral and is not found in the atmosphere. Fungi and plant roots have a structure called mycorrhizae that are able to fix insoluble phosphates into useable phosphorus. Urine and decayed matter return phosphorus to the earth where it can be fixed in the plant. Phosphorus is needed for the backbone of DNA and for ATP manufacturing.

Biogeochemical cycling is the movement of chemicals between the biotic (living) and abiotic (non-living) parts of an ecosystem. Respiration and photosynthesis play an important role in the cycling of oxygen and carbon. Respiration is the process in which an individual organism uses oxygen and releases carbon dioxide to the atmosphere during energy producing reactions. Photosynthesis, the reverse of respiration, is the process in which an individual plant or microorganism uses the carbon from carbon dioxide to produce carbohydrates with oxygen as a by-product.

Two major forms of carbon in the environment are carbon dioxide gas in the atmosphere and organic macromolecules in living things. Photosynthesis by plants and microorganisms converts carbon dioxide to carbohydrates, removing carbon from the atmosphere and storing it as biomass. Conversely, aerobic and anaerobic respiration by plants, animals, and microorganisms returns carbon to the environment in the form of carbon dioxide or methane gas, respectively.

The main driving force in the oxygen cycle is photosynthesis. Plants and microorganisms perform photosynthesis to produce glucose, releasing oxygen gas to the environment as a by-product. Animals, plants, and microorganisms remove oxygen from the environment, using it to break down glucose in an energy yielding reaction that produces carbon dioxide and water.

Skill 28.4 Evaluate the effects of limiting factors on ecosystem productivity (e.g., light intensity, gas concentrations, mineral availability).

A limiting factor is the component of a biological process that determines how quickly or slowly the process proceeds. Photosynthesis is the main biological process determining the rate of ecosystem productivity, the rate at which an ecosystem creates biomass. Thus, in evaluating the productivity of an ecosystem, potential limiting factors are light intensity, gas concentrations, and mineral availability. The Law of the Minimum states that the required factor in a given process that is most scarce controls the rate of the process.

One potential limiting factor of ecosystem productivity is light intensity because photosynthesis requires light energy. Light intensity can limit productivity in two ways. First, too little light limits the rate of photosynthesis because the required energy is not available. Second, too much light can damage the photosynthetic system of plants and microorganisms thus slowing the rate of photosynthesis. Decreased photosynthesis equals decreased productivity.

Another potential limiting factor of ecosystem productivity is gas concentrations. Photosynthesis requires carbon dioxide. Thus, increased concentration of carbon dioxide often results in increased productivity. While carbon dioxide is often not the ultimate limiting factor of productivity, increased concentration can indirectly increase rates of photosynthesis in several ways. First, increased carbon dioxide concentration often increases the rate of nitrogen fixation (available nitrogen is another limiting factor of productivity). Second, increased carbon dioxide concentration can decrease the pH of rain, improving the water source of photosynthetic organisms.

Finally, mineral availability also limits ecosystem productivity. Plants require adequate amounts of nitrogen and phosphorus to build many cellular structures. The availability of the inorganic minerals phosphorus and nitrogen often is the main limiting factor of plant biomass production. In other words, in a natural environment phosphorus and nitrogen availability most often limits ecosystem productivity, rather than carbon dioxide concentration or light intensity.

Competency 0029

Understand concepts of human ecology and the impact of human decisions and activities on the abiotic and biotic environments.

Skill 29.1 Recognize the importance and implications of influencing factors (e.g., nutrition, public health) on human population dynamics.

The human population has been growing exponentially for centuries. People are living longer and healthier lives than ever before. Better health care and nutrition practices have helped in the survival of the population.

Human activity affects parts of the nutrient cycles by removing nutrients from one part of the biosphere and adding them to another. This results in nutrient depletion in one area and nutrient excess in another. This affects water systems, crops, wildlife, and humans.

Humans are responsible for the depletion of the ozone layer. This depletion is due to chemicals used for refrigeration and aerosols. The consequences of ozone depletion will be severe. Ozone protects the Earth from the majority of UV radiation. An increase of UV will promote skin cancer and unknown effects on wildlife and plants.

Skill 29.2 Predict the impact of human use of natural resources (e.g., forests, rivers) on organisms.

Humans have a tremendous impact on the world's natural resources. The world's natural water supplies are affected by human use. Waterways are major sources for recreation and freight transportation. Oil and wastes from boats and cargo ships pollute the aquatic environment. The aquatic plant and animal life is affected by this contamination.

Deforestation for urban development has resulted in the extinction or relocation of several species of plants and animals. Animals are forced to leave their forest homes or perish amongst the destruction. The number of plant and animal species that have become extinct due to deforestation is unknown. Scientists have only identified a fraction of the species on Earth. It is known that if the destruction of natural resources continues, there may be no plants or animals successfully reproducing in the wild.

Skill 29.3 Analyze types of resource misuse and their long- and short-term effects.

The two categories of natural resources are renewable and nonrenewable. Renewable resources are unlimited because they can be replaced as they are used. Examples of renewable resources are oxygen, wood, fresh water, and biomass. Nonrenewable resources are present in finite amounts or are used faster than they can be replaced in nature. Examples of nonrenewable resources are petroleum, coal, and natural gas.

Strategies for the management of renewable resources focus on balancing the immediate demand for resources with long-term sustainability. In addition, renewable resource management attempts to optimize the quality of the resources. For example, scientists may attempt to manage the amount of timber harvested from a forest, balancing the human need for wood with the future viability of the forest as a source of wood. Scientists attempt to increase timber production by fertilizing, manipulating trees genetically, and managing pests and density. Similar strategies exist for the management and optimization of water sources, air quality, and other plants and animals.

The main concerns in nonrenewable resource management are conservation, allocation, and environmental mitigation. Policy makers, corporations, and governments must determine how to use and distribute scare resources. Decision makers must balance the immediate demand for resources with the need for resources in the future. This determination is often the cause of conflict and disagreement. Finally, scientists attempt to minimize and mitigate the environmental damage caused by resource extraction. Scientists devise methods of harvesting and using resources that do not unnecessarily impact the environment. After the extraction of resources from a location, scientists devise plans and methods to restore the environment to as close to its original state as possible.

Skill 29.4 Evaluate methods and technologies that reduce or mitigate environmental degradation.

Environmental degradation is damage to an ecosystem, or the biosphere as a whole, resulting from human activities. The underlying causes of environmental degradation are production of energy and consumer products, human population growth and development, and waste disposal. Production of energy and consumer products pollutes the air and contributes to global warming. In addition, harvesting of natural resources can deplete supplies and damage ecosystems. Growth and development of human communities can diminish natural resource supplies, damage the land, and disrupt natural ecosystems. Finally, improper waste disposal can pollute the land and water supplies.

Scientists and policy makers continually attempt to develop and implement new methods and technologies to reduce or mitigate environmental degradation. Cleaner burning fuels or alternative sources of energy that do not pollute the air potential solutions to the energy production-air pollution trade off. In addition, the treatment and filtering of fuel burning by-products can limit environmental impact. However, both developing alternative energy sources and treating current emissions are costly processes. In a market driven economy, governments and policy makers must provide incentives and implement regulations to encourage and require environmental responsibility.

Growth and development of human communities, while inevitable, requires careful planning and attention to environmental concerns. Governmental regulations are often necessary to limit the affect of growth on surrounding ecosystems. Developers and policy makers must attempt to balance the need for increased housing and construction with the importance of respecting and maintaining biodiversity and ecosystem function.

Finally, improper waste disposal can pollute the land and water. Many human and industrial waste products are highly toxic and can cause irreversible environmental damage. Methods of reducing environmental degradation resulting from waste disposal include careful treatment of sewage and human waste, safe disposal of waste products in properly designed locations, and recycling and reuse of waste products.

TEACHER CERTIFICATION STUDY GUIDE

Sample Test

Directions: Read each item and select the best response.

1. A student designed a science project testing the effects of light and water on plant growth. You would recommend that she

   A. manipulate the temperature as well.

   B. also alter the pH of the water as another variable.

   C. omit either water or light as a variable.

   D. also alter the light concentration as another variable.

2. Identify the control in the following experiment. A student had four plants grown under the following conditions and was measuring photosynthetic rate by measuring mass. 2 plants in 50% light and 2 plants in 100% light.

   A. plants grown with no added nutrients

   B. plants grown in the dark

   C plants in 100% light

   D. plants in 50% light

3. In an experiment measuring the growth of bacteria at different temperatures, identify the independent variable.

   A. growth of number of colonies

   B. temperature

   C. type of bacteria used

   D. light intensity

4. A scientific theory

   A. proves scientific accuracy.
   B. is never rejected.
   C. results in a medical breakthrough.
   D. may be altered at a later time.

5. Which is the correct order of methodology? 1) testing revised explanation, 2) setting up a controlled experiment to test explanation, 3) drawing a conclusion, 4) suggesting an explanation for observations, and 5) compare observed results to hypothesized results

   A. 4, 2, 3, 1, 5

   B. 3, 1, 4, 2, 5

   C. 4, 2, 5, 1, 3

   D. 2, 5, 4, 1, 3

BIOLOGICAL SCIENCES

6. Given a choice, which is the most desirable method of heating a substance in the lab?

   A. alcohol burner

   B. gas burner

   C. bunsen burner

   D. hot plate

7. Biological waste should be disposed of

   A. in the trash can.

   B. under a fume hood.

   C. in the broken glass box.

   D. in an autoclavable biohazard bag.

8. Chemicals should be stored

   A. in a cool dark room.

   B. in a dark room.

   C. according to their reactivity with other substances.

   D. in a double locked room.

9. Given the choice of lab activities, which would you omit?

   A. a genetics experiment tracking the fur color of mice

   B. dissecting a preserved fetal pig

   C. a lab relating temperature to respiration rate using live goldfish.

   D. pithing a frog to see the action of circulation

10. Who should be notified in the case of a serious chemical spill?

    I. the custodian
    II. The fire department
    III. the chemistry teacher
    IV. the administration

    A. I

    B. II

    C. II and III

    D. II and IV

11. The "Right to Know" law states

    A. the inventory of toxic chemicals checked against the "Substance List" be available.

    B. that students are to be informed on alternatives to dissection.

    C. that science teachers are to be informed of student allergies.

    D. that students are to be informed of infectious microorganisms used in lab.

12. In which situation would a science teacher be liable?

    A. a teacher leaves to receive an emergency phone call and a student slips and falls.

    B. a student removes their goggles and gets dissection fluid in their eye.

    C. a faulty gas line results in a fire.

    D. a students cuts themselves with a scalpel.

13. Which statement best defines negligence?

    A. failure to give oral instructions for those with reading disabilities

    B. failure to exercise ordinary care

    C. inability to supervise a large group of students.

    D. reasonable anticipation that an event may occur

14. Which item should always be used when using chemicals with noxious vapors?

    A. eye protection

    B. face shield

    C. fume hood

    D. lab apron

15. Identify the correct sequence of organization of living things.

    A. cell – organelle – organ – tissue – organ system – organism

    B. cell – tissue – organ – organelle – organ system – organism

    C. organelle – cell – tissue – organ – organ system – organism

    D. organ system – tissue – organelle – cell – organism – organ

16. Which is not a characteristic of living things?

    A. movement

    B. cellular structure

    C. metabolism

    D. reproduction

17. Which kingdom is comprised of organisms made of one cell with no nuclear membrane?

    A. Monera

    B. Protista

    C. Fungi

    D. Algae

18. Potassium chloride is an example of a(n)

    A. non polar covalent bond

    B. polar covalent bond

    C. ionic bond

    D. hydrogen bond

19. Which of the following is a monomer?

    A. RNA

    B. glycogen

    C. DNA

    D. amino acid

20. Which of the following are properties of water?

    I. High specific heat
    II. Strong ionic bonds
    III. Good solvent
    IV. High freezing point

    A. I, III, IV

    B. II and III

    C. I and II

    D. II, III, IV

BIOLOGICAL SCIENCES

21. Which does not affect enzyme rate?

    A. increase of temperature

    B. amount of substrate

    C. pH

    D. size of the cell

22. Sulfur oxides and nitrogen oxides in the environment react with water to cause

    A. ammonia

    B. acidic precipitation

    C. sulfuric acid

    D. global warming

23. The loss of an electron is _____ and the gain of an electron is _____.

    A. oxidation, reduction

    B. reduction, oxidation

    C. glycolysis, photosynthesis

    D. photosynthesis, glycolysis

24. The product of anaerobic respiration in animals is

    A. carbon dioxide

    B. lactic acid

    C. pyruvate

    D. ethyl alcohol

25. In the comparison of respiration to photosynthesis, which statement is true?

    A. oxygen is a waste product in photosynthesis but not in respiration

    B. glucose is produced in respiration but not in photosynthesis

    C. carbon dioxide is formed in photosynthesis but not in respiration

    D. water is formed in respiration but not in photosynthesis

26. Carbon dioxide is fixed in the form of glucose in

    A. Krebs cycle

    B. the light reactions

    C. the dark reactions (Calvin cycle)

    D. glycolysis

27. During the Kreb's cycle, 8 carrier molecules are formed. What are they?

    A. 3 NADH, 3 FADH, 2 ATP

    B. 6 NADH and 2 ATP

    C. 4 $FADH_2$ and 4 ATP

    D. 6 NADH and 2 $FADH_2$

28. Which of the following is not posttranscriptional processing?

    A. 5' capping

    B. intron splicing

    C. polypeptide splicing

    D. 3' polyadenylation

29. Polymerase chain reaction

    A. is a group of polymerases

    B. technique for amplifying DNA

    C. primer for DNA synthesis

    D. synthesis of polymerase

30. Homozygous individuals

    A. have two different alleles

    B. are of the same species

    C. have the same features

    D. have a pair of identical alleles

31. The two major ways to determine taxonomic classification are

    A. evolution and phylogeny

    B. reproductive success and evolution

    C. phylogeny and morphology

    D. size and color

32. Man's scientific name is Homo sapiens. Choose the proper classification beginning with kingdom and ending with order.

    A. Animalia, Vertebrata, Mammalia, Primate, Hominidae

    B. Animalia, Vertebrata, Chordata, Mammalia, Primate

    C. Animalia, Chordata, Vertebrata, Mammalia, Primate

    D. Chordata, Vertebrata, Primate, Homo, sapiens

33. The scientific name Canis familiaris refers to the animal's

    A. kingdom and phylum names

    B. genus and species names

    C. class and species names

    D. order and family names

34. Members of the same species

    A. look identical

    B. never change

    C. reproduce successfully among their group

    D. live in the same geographic location

35. What is necessary for diffusion to occur?

    A. carrier proteins

    B. energy

    C. a concentration gradient

    D. a membrane

36. Which is an example of the use of energy to move a substance through a membrane from areas of low concentration to areas of high concentration?

    A. osmosis

    B. active transport

    C. exocytosis

    D. phagocytosis

37. A plant cell is placed in salt water. The resulting movement of water out of the cell is called

    A. facilitated diffusion

    B. diffusion

    C. transpiration

    D. osmosis

38. As the amount of waste production increases in a cell, the rate of excretion

    A. slowly decreases

    B. remains the same

    C. increases

    D. stops due to cell death

39. A type of molecule not found in the membrane of an animal cell is

    A. phospholipid

    B. protein

    C. cellulose

    D. cholesterol

40. Which type of cell would contain the most mitochondria?

    A. muscle cell

    B. nerve cell

    C. epithelium

    D. blood cell

41. The first cells that evolved on earth were probably of which type?

    A. autotrophs

    B. eukaryotes

    C. heterotrophs

    D. prokaryotes

42. According to the fluid-mosaic model of the cell membrane, membranes are composed of

    A. phospholipid bilayers with proteins embedded in the layers

    B. one layer of phospholipids with cholesterol embedded in the layer

    C. two layers of protein with lipids embedded the the layers

    D. DNA and fluid proteins

43. All the following statements regarding both a mitochondria and a chloroplast are correct except

    A. they both produce energy over a gradient

    B. they both have DNA and are capable of reproduction

    C. they both transfer light energy to chemical energy

    D. they both make ATP

44. This stage of mitosis includes cytokinesis or division of the cytoplasm and its organelles

    A. anaphase

    B. interphase

    C. prophase

    D. telophase

45. Replication of chromosomes occurs during which phase of the cell cycle?

    A. prophase

    B. interphase

    C. metaphase

    D. anaphase

46. Which statement regarding mitosis is correct?

    A. diploid cells produce haploid cells for sexual reproduction

    B. sperm and egg cells are produced

    C. diploid cells produce diploid cells for growth and repair

    D. it allows for greater genetic diversity

47. In a plant cell, telophase is described as

    A. the time of chromosome doubling

    B. cell plate formation

    C. the time when crossing over occurs

    D. cleavage furrow formation

48. Identify this stage of mitosis

    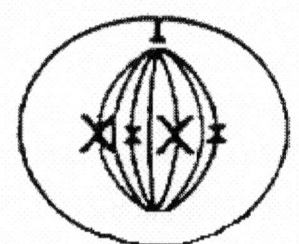

    A. anaphase

    B. metaphase

    C. telophase

    D. prophase

49. Identify this stage of mitosis

    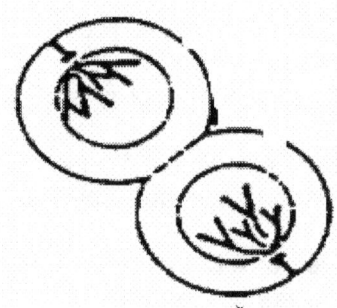

    A. prophase

    B. telophase

    C. anaphase

    D. metaphase

50. Identify this stage of mitosis

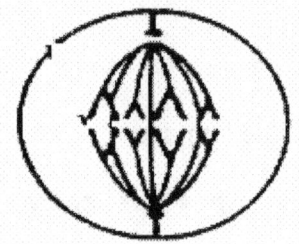

A. anaphase

B. metaphase

C. prophase

D. telophase

51. Oxygen is given off in the

A. light reactions of photosynthesis

B. dark reactions of photosynthesis

C. Kreb's cycle

D. reduction of NAD+ to NADH

52. In the electron transport chain, all the following are true except

A. it occurs in the mitochondrion

B. it does not make ATP directly

C. the net gain of energy is 30 ATP

D. most molecules in the electron transport chain are proteins.

53. The area of a DNA nucleotide that varies is the

A. deoxyribose

B. phosphate group

C. nitrogen base

D. sugar

54. A DNA strand has the base sequence of TCAGTA. Its DNA complement would have the following sequence

A. ATGACT

B. TCAGTA

C. AGUCAU

D. AGTCAT

55. Genes function in specifying the structure of which molecule?

A. carbohydrates

B. lipids

C. nucleic acids

D. proteins

56. What is the correct order of steps in protein synthesis?

A. transcription, then replication

B. transcription, then translation

C. translation, then transcription

D. replication, then translation

57. This carries amino acids to the ribosome in protein synthesis

A. messenger RNA

B. ribosomal RNA

C. transfer RNA

D. DNA

58. A protein is sixty amino acids in length. This requires a coded DNA sequence of how many nucleotides?

    A. 20

    B. 30

    C. 120

    D. 180

59. A DNA molecule has the sequence of ACTATG. What is the anticodon of this molecule?

    A. UGAUAC

    B. ACUAUG

    C. TGATAC

    D. ACTATG

60. The term "phenotype" refers to which of the following?

    A. a condition which is heterozygous

    B. the genetic makeup of an individual

    C. a condition which is homozygous

    D. how the genotype is expressed

61. The ratio of brown-eyed to blue-eyed children from the mating of a blue-eyed male to a heterozygous brown-eyed female would be expected to be which of the following?

    A. 2:1

    B. 1:1

    C. 1:0

    D. 1:2

62. The Law of Segregation defined by Mendel states that

    A. when sex cells form, the two alleles that determine a trait will end up on different gametes

    B. only one of two alleles is expressed in a heterozygous organism

    C. the allele expressed is the dominant allele

    D. alleles of one trait do not affect the inheritance of alleles on another chromosome

63. When a white flower is crossed with a red flower, incomplete dominance can be seen by the production of which of the following?

    A. pink flowers

    B. red flowers

    C. white flowers

    D. red and white flowers

64. Sutton observed that genes and chromosomes behaved the same. This led him to his theory which stated

    A. that meiosis causes chromosome separation

    B. that linked genes are able to separate

    C. that genes and chromosomes have the same function

    D. that genes are found on chromosomes

65. Amniocentesis is

    A. a non-invasive technique for detecting genetic disorders

    B. a bacterial infection

    C. extraction of amniotic fluid

    D. removal of fetal tissue

66. A child with type O blood has a father with type A blood and a mother with type B blood. The genotypes of the parents respectively would be which of the following?

    A. AA and BO

    B. AO and BO

    C. AA and BB

    D. AO and OO

67. Any change that affects the sequence of bases in a gene is called a (n)

    A. deletion

    B. polyploid

    C. mutation

    D. duplication

68. The *lac* operon

    I. contains the *lac Z, lac Y, lac A* genes
    II. converts glucose to lactose
    III. contains a repressor
    IV. is on when the repressor is activated

    A. I

    B. II

    C. III and IV

    D. I and III

69. Which of the following factors will affect the Hardy-Weinberg law of equilibrium, leading to evolutionary change?

    A. no mutations

    B. non-random mating

    C. no immigration or emigration

    D. Large population

70. If a population is in Hardy-Weinberg equilibrium and the frequency of the recessive allele is .3, what percentage of the population would be expected to be heterozygous?

    A. 9%

    B. 49%

    C. 42%

    D. 21%

71. Crossing over, which increases genetic diversity occurs during which stage(s)?

    A. telophase II in meiosis

    B. metaphase in mitosis

    C. interphase in both mitosis and meiosis

    D. prophase I in meiosis

72. Cancer cells divide extensively and invade other tissues. This continuous cell division is due to

    A. density dependent inhibition

    B. density independent inhibition

    C. chromosome replication

    D. Growth factors

73. Which process(es) results in a haploid chromosome number?

    A. both meiosis and mitosis

    B. mitosis

    C. meiosis

    D. replication and division

74. Segments of DNA can be transferred from the DNA of one organism to another through the use of which of the following?

    A. bacterial plasmids

    B. viruses

    C. chromosomes from frogs

    D. plant DNA

75. Which of the following is not true regarding restriction enzymes?

    A. they do not aid in recombination procedures

    B. they are used in genetic engineering

    C. they are named after the bacteria in which they naturally occur

    D. they identify and splice certain base sequences on DNA

76. A virus that can remain dormant until a certain environmental condition causes its rapid increase is said to be

    A. lytic

    B. benign

    C. saprophytic

    D. lysogenic

77. Which is not considered to be a morphological type of bacteria?

    A. obligate

    B. coccus

    C. spirillum

    D. bacillus

78. Antibiotics are effective in fighting bacterial infections due to their ability to

    A. interfere with DNA replication in the bacteria

    B. prevent the formation of new cell walls in the bacteria

    C. disrupt the ribosome of the bacteria

    D. All of the above.

79. Bacteria commonly reproduce by a process called binary fission. Which of the following best defines this process?

   A. viral vectors carry DNA to new bacteria

   B. DNA from one bacterium enters another

   C. DNA doubles and the bacterial cell divides

   D. DNA from dead cells is absorbed into bacteria

80. All of the following are examples of a member of Kingdom Fungi except

   A. mold

   B. algae

   C. mildew

   D. mushrooms

81. Protists are classified into major groups according to

   A. their method of obtaining nutrition

   B. reproduction

   C. metabolism

   D. their form and function

82. In comparison to protist cells, moneran cells

   I. are usually smaller
   II. evolved later
   III. are more complex
   IV. contain more organelles

   A. I

   B. I and II

   C. II and III

   D. I and IV

83. Spores characterize the reproduction mode for which of the following group of plants?

   A. algae

   B. flowering plants

   C. conifers

   D. ferns

84. Water movement to the top of a twenty foot tree is most likely due to which principle?

   A. osmostic pressure

   B. xylem pressure

   C. capillarity

   D. transpiration

85. What are the stages of development from the egg to the plant?

   A. morphogenesis, growth, and cellular differentiation

   B. cell differentiation, growth, and morphogenesis

   C. growth, morphogenesis, and cellular differentiation

   D. growth, cellular differentiation, and morphogensis

86. In angiosperms, the food for the developing plant is found in which of the following structures?

   A. ovule

   B. endosperm

   C. male gametophyte

   D. cotyledon

87. The process in which pollen grains are released from the anthers is called

   A. pollination

   B. fertilization

   C. blooming

   D. dispersal

88. Which of the following is not a characteristic of a monocot?

   A. parallel veins in leaves

   B. petals of flowers occur in multiples of 4 or 5

   C. one seed leaf

   D. vascular tissue scattered throughout the stem

89. What controls gas exchange on the bottom of a plant leaf?

   A. stomata

   B. epidermis

   C. collenchyma and schlerenchyma

   D. palisade mesophyll

90. How are angiosperms different from other groups of plants?

   A. presence of flowers and fruits

   B. production of spores for reproduction

   C. true roots and stems

   D. seed production

91. Generations of plants alternate between

   A. angiosperms and bryophytes

   B. flowering and nonflowering stages

   C. seed bearing and spore bearing plants

   D. haploid and diploid stages

92. Double fertilization refers to which choice of the following?

   A. two sperm fertilizing one egg

   B. fertilization of a plant by gametes from two separate plants

   C. two sperm enter the plant embryo sac; one sperm fertilizes the egg, the other forms the endosperm

   D. the production of non-identical twins through fertilization of two separate eggs

93. Characteristics of coelomates include:

   I. no true digestive system
   II. two germ layers
   III. true fluid filled cavity
   IV. three germ layers

   A. I

   B. II and IV

   C. IV

   D. III and IV

94. Which phylum accounts for 85% of all animal species?

   A. Nematoda

   B. Chordata

   C. Arthropoda

   D. Cnidaria

95. Which is the correct statement regarding the human nervous system and the human endocrine system?

   A. the nervous system maintains homeostasis whereas the endocrine system does not

   B. endocrine glands produce neurotransmitters whereas nerves produce hormones

   C. nerve signals travel on neurons whereas hormones travel through the blood

   D. he nervous system involves chemical transmission whereas the endocrine system does not

96. A muscular adaptation to move food through the digestive system is called

   A. peristalsis

   B. passive transport

   C. voluntary action

   D. bulk transport

97. The role of neurotransmitters in nerve action is

   A. turn off sodium pump

   B. turn off calcium pump

   C. send impulse to neuron

   D. send impulse to the body

98. Fats are broken down by which substance?

   A. bile produced in the gall bladder

   B. lipase produced in the gall bladder

   C. glucagons produced in the liver

   D. bile produced in the liver

99. Fertilization in humans usually occurs in the

   A. uterus

   B. ovary

   C. fallopian tubes

   D. vagina

100. All of the following are found in the dermis layer of skin except

    A. sweat glands

    B. keratin

    C. hair follicles

    D. blood vessels

101. Which is the correct sequence of embryonic development in a frog?

    A. cleavage – blastula – gastrula

    B. cleavage – gastrula – blastula

    C. blastula – cleavage – gastrula

    D. gastrula – blastula – cleavage

102. Food is carried through the digestive tract by a series of wave-like contractions. This process is called

    A. peristalsis

    B. chyme

    C. digestion

    D. absorption

103. Movement is possible by the action of muscles pulling on

    A. skin

    B. bones

    C. joints

    D. ligaments

104. All of the following are functions of the skin except

    A. storage

    B. protection

    C. sensation

    D. regulation of temperature

105. Hormones are essential to the regulation of reproduction. What organ is responsible for the release of hormones for sexual maturity?

    A. pituitary gland

    B. hypothalamus

    C. pancreas

    D. thyroid gland

106. A bicyclist has a heart rate of 110 beats per minute and a stroke volume of 85 mL per beat. What is the cardiac output?

    A. 9.35 L/min

    B. 1.29 L/min

    C. 0.772 L/min

    D. 129 L/min

107. After sea turtles are hatched on the beach, they start the journey to the ocean. This is due to

    A. innate behavior

    B. territoriality

    C. the tide

    D. learned behavior

108. A school age boy had the chicken pox as a baby. He will most likely not get this disease again because of

   A. passive immunity
   B. vaccination
   C. antibiotics
   D. active immunity

109. High humidity and temperature stability are present in which of the following biomes?

   A. taiga
   B. deciduous forest
   C. desert
   D. tropical rain forest

110. The biological species concept applies to

   A. asexual organisms
   B. extinct organisms
   C. sexual organisms
   D. fossil organisms

111. Which term is not associated with the water cycle?

   A. precipitation
   B. transpiration
   C. fixation
   D. evaporation

112. All of the following are density independent factors that affect a population except

   A. temperature
   B. rainfall
   C. predation
   D. soil nutrients

113. In the growth of a population, the increase is exponential until carrying capacity is reached. This is represented by a (n)

   A. S curve
   B. J curve
   C. M curve
   D. L curve

114. Primary succession occurs after

   A. nutrient enrichment
   B. a forest fire
   C. bare rock is exposed after a water table recedes
   D. a housing development is built

115. Crabgrass – grasshopper – frog – snake – eagle If DDT were present in an ecosystem, which organism would have the highest concentration in its system?

   A. grasshopper
   B. eagle
   C. frog
   D. crabgrass

116. Which trophic level has the highest ecological efficiency?

   A. decomposers

   B. producers

   C. tertiary consumers

   D. secondary consumers

117. A clownfish is protected by the sea anemone's tentacles. In turn, the anemone receives uneaten food from the clownfish. This is an example of

   A. mutualism

   B. parasitism

   C. commensalisms

   D. competition

118. If the niches of two species overlap, what usually results?

   A. a symbiotic relationship

   B. cooperation

   C. competition

   D. a new species

119. Oxygen created in photosynthesis comes from the breakdown of

   A. carbon dioxide

   B. water

   C. glucose

   D. carbon monoxide

120. Which photosystem makes ATP?

   A. photosystem I

   B. photosystem II

   C. photosystem III

   D. photosystem IV

121. All of the following gasses made up the primitive atmosphere except

   A. ammonia

   B. methane

   C. oxygen

   D. hydrogen

122. The Endosymbiotic theory states that

   A. eukaryotes arose from prokaryotes

   B. animals evolved in close relationships with one another

   C. the prokaryotes arose from eukaryotes

   D. life arose from inorganic compounds

123. Which aspect of science does not support evolution?

   A. comparative anatomy

   B. organic chemistry

   C. comparison of DNA among organisms

   D. analogous structures

124. Evolution occurs in

A. individuals

B. populations

C. organ systems

D. cells

125. Which process contributes to the large variety of living things in the world today?

A. meiosis

B. asexual reproduction

C. mitosis

D. alternation of generations

126. The wing of bird, human arm and whale flipper have the same bone structure. These are called

A. polymorphic structures

B. homologous structures

C. vestigial structures

D. analogous structures

127. Which biome is the most prevalent on Earth?

A. marine

B. desert

C. savanna

D. tundra

128. Which of the following is not an abiotic factor?

A. temperature

B. rainfall

C. soil quality

D. bacteria

129. DNA synthesis results in a strand that is synthesized continuously. This is the

A. lagging strand

B. leading strand

C. template strand

D. complementary strand

130. Using a gram staining technique, it is observed that E. coli stains pink. It is therefore

A. gram positive

B. dead

C. gram negative

D. gram neutral

131. A light microscope has an ocular of 10X and an objective of 40X. What is the total magnification?

A. 400X

B. 30X

C. 50X

D. 4000X

132. Three plants were grown. The following data was taken. Determine the mean growth.
Plant 1: 10cm Plant 2: 20cm Plant 3: 15cm

   A. 5 cm

   B. 45 cm

   C. 12 cm

   D. 15 cm

133. Electrophoresis separates DNA on the basis of

   A. amount of current

   B. molecular size

   C. positive charge of the molecule

   D. solubility of the gel

134. The reading of a meniscus in a graduated cylinder is done at the

   A. top of the meniscus

   B. middle of the meniscus

   C. bottom of the meniscus

   D. closest whole number

135. Two hundred plants were grown. Fifty plants died. What percentage of the plants survived?

   A. 40%

   B. 25%

   C. 75%

   D. 50%

136. Which is not a correct statement regarding the use of a light microscope?

   A. carry the microscope with two hands

   B. store on the low power objective

   C. clean all lenses with lens paper

   D. Focus first on high power

137. Spectrophotometry utilizes the principle of

   A. light transmission

   B. molecular weight

   C. solubility of the substance

   D. electrical charges

138. Chromotography is most often associated with the separation of

   A. nutritional elements

   B. DNA

   C. proteins

   D. plant pigments

139. A genetic engineering advancement in the medical field is

   A. gene therapy

   B. pesticides

   C. degradation of harmful chemicals

   D. antibiotics

140. Which scientists are credited with the discovery of the structure of DNA?

    A. Hershey & Chase
    B. Sutton & Morgan
    C. Watson & Crick
    D. Miller & Fox

141. Negatively charged particles that circle the nucleus of an atom are called

    A. neutrons
    B. neutrinos
    C. electrons
    D. protons

142. The shape of a cell depends on its

    A. function
    B. structure
    C. age
    D. size

143. The most ATP is generated through

    A. fermentation
    B. glycolysis
    C. chemiosmosis
    D. Krebs cycle

144. In DNA, adenine bonds with _____, while cytosine bonds with _____.

    A. thymine/guanine
    B. adenine/cytosine
    C. cytosine/adenine
    D. guanine/thymine

145. The individual parts of cells are best studied using a (n)

    A. ultracentrifuge
    B. phase-contrast microscope
    C. CAT scan
    D. electron microscope

146. Thermoacidophiles are

    A. prokaryotes
    B. eukaryotes
    C. bacteria
    D. archaea

147. Which of the following is not a type of fiber that makes up the cytoskeleton?

    A. vacuoles
    B. microfilaments
    C. microtubules
    D. intermediate filaments

148. Viruses are made of

A. a protein coat surrounding a nucleic acid

B. DNA, RNA and a cell wall

C. a nucleic acid surrounding a protein coat

D. protein surrounded by DNA

149. Reproductive isolation results in

A. extinction

B. migration

C. follilization

D. speciation

150. This protein structure consists of the coils and folds of polypeptide chains. Which is it?

A. secondary structure

B. quaternary structure

C. tertiary structure

D. primary structure

Answer Key

1. C	31. C	61. B	91. D	121. C
2. C	32. C	62. A	92. C	122. A
3. B	33. B	63. A	93. D	123. B
4. D	34. C	64. D	94. C	124. B
5. C	35. C	65. C	95. C	125. A
6. D	36. B	66. B	96. A	126. B
7. D	37. D	67. C	97. A	127. A
8. C	38. C	68. D	98. D	128. D
9. D	39. C	69. B	99. C	129. B
10. D	40. A	70. C	100. B	130. C
11. A	41. D	71. D	101. A	131. A
12. A	42. A	72. B	102. A	132. D
13. B	43. C	73. C	103. B	133. B
14. C	44. D	74. A	104. A	134. C
15. C	45. B	75. A	105. B	135. C
16. A	46. C	76. D	106. A	136. D
17. A	47. B	77. A	107. A	137. A
18. C	48. B	78. D	108. D	138. D
19. D	49. B	79. C	109. D	139. A
20. A	50. A	80. B	110. C	140. C
21. D	51. A	81. D	111. C	141. C
22. B	52. C	82. A	112. C	142. A
23. A	53. C	83. D	113. A	143. C
24. B	54. D	84. D	114. C	144. A
25. A	55. D	85. C	115. B	145. D
26. C	56. B	86. B	116. B	146. D
27. D	57. C	87. A	117. A	147. A
28. C	58. D	88. B	118. C	148. A
29. B	59. B	89. A	119. B	149. D
30. D	60. D	90. A	120. A	150. A

Rationales for Sample Questions

1. A student designed a science project testing the effects of light and water on plant growth. You would recommend that she:

    A. manipulate the temperature as well.
    B. also alter the pH of the water as another variable.
    C. omit either water or light as a variable.
    D. also alter the light concentration as another variable.

C. In science, experiments should be designed so that only one variable is manipulated at a time.

2. Identify the control in the following experiment. A student had four plants grown under the following conditions and was measuring photosynthetic rate by measuring mass. 2 plants in 50% light and 2 plants in 100% light.

    A. plants grown with no added nutrients
    B. plants grown in the dark
    C plants in 100% light
    D. plants in 50% light

C. The 100% light plants are those that the student will be comparing the 50% plants to. This will be the control.

3. In an experiment measuring the growth of bacteria at different temperatures, identify the independent variable.

    A. growth of number of colonies
    B. temperature
    C. type of bacteria used
    D. light intensity

B. The independent variable is controlled by the experimenter. Here, the temperature is controlled to determine its effect on the growth of bacteria (dependent variable).

4. A scientific theory

    A. proves scientific accuracy.
    B. is never rejected.
    C. results in a medical breakthrough.
    D. may be altered at a later time.

D. Scientific theory is usually accepted and verified information but can always be changed at anytime.

5. Which is the correct order of methodology? 1) testing revised explanation, 2) setting up a controlled experiment to test explanation, 3) drawing a conclusion, 4) suggesting an explanation for observations, and 5) compare observed results to hypothesized results

    A. 4, 2, 3, 1, 5
    B. 3, 1, 4, 2, 5
    C. 4, 2, 5, 1, 3
    D. 2, 5, 4, 1, 3

C. The first step in scientific inquiry is posing a question to be answered. Next, a hypothesis is formed to provide a plausible explanation. An experiment is then proposed and performed to test this hypothesis. A comparison between the predicted and observed results is the next step. Conclusions are then formed and it is determined whether the hypothesis is correct or incorrect. If incorrect, the next step is to form a new hypothesis and the process is repeated.

6. Given a choice, which is the most desirable method of heating a substance in the lab?

    A. alcohol burner
    B. gas burner
    C. bunsen burner
    D. hot plate

D. A hotplate is the only heat source from the choices above that does not have an open flame. The use of a hot plate will reduce the risk of fire and injury to students.

7. Biological waste should be disposed of

A. in the trash can.
B. under a fume hood.
C. in the broken glass box.
D. in an autoclavable biohazard bag.

D. Biological material should never be stored near food or water used for human consumption. All biological material should be appropriately labeled. All blood and body fluids should be put in a well-contained container with a secure lid to prevent leaking. All biological waste should be disposed of in biological hazardous waste bags.

8. Chemicals should be stored

A. in a cool dark room.
B. in a dark room.
C. according to their reactivity with other substances.
D. in a double locked room.

C. All chemicals should be stored with other chemicals of similar reactivity. Failure to do so could result in an undesirable chemical reaction.

9. Given the choice of lab activities, which would you omit?

A. a genetics experiment tracking the fur color of mice
B. dissecting a preserved fetal pig
C. a lab relating temperature to respiration rate using live goldfish.
D. pithing a frog to see the action of circulation

D. The use of live vertebrate organisms in a way that may harm the animal is prohibited. The observation of fur color in mice is not harmful to the animal and the use of live goldfish is acceptable because they are invertebrates. The dissection of a fetal pig is acceptable if it comes from a known origin.

10. Who should be notified in the case of a serious chemical spill?

    I. the custodian
    II. The fire department
    III. the chemistry teacher
    IV. the administration

    A. I
    B. II
    C. II and III
    D. II and IV

D. For large spills, the school administration and the local fire department should be notified.

11. The "Right to Know" law   states

    A. the inventory of toxic chemicals checked against the "Substance List" be available.
    B. that students are to be informed on alternatives to dissection.
    C. that science teachers are to be informed of student allergies.
    D. that students are to be informed of infectious microorganisms used in lab.

A. The right to know law pertains to chemical substances in the lab. Employees should check the material safety data sheets and the substance list for potential hazards in the lab.

12. In which situation would a science teacher be liable?

    A. a teacher leaves to receive an emergency phone call and a student slips and falls.
    B. a student removes their goggles and gets dissection fluid in their eye.
    C. a faulty gas line results in a fire.
    D. a students cuts themselves with a scalpel.

A. A teacher has an obligation to be present in the lab at all times. If the teacher needs to leave, an appropriate substitute is needed.

13. Which statement best defines negligence?

    A. failure to give oral instructions for those with reading disabilities
    B. failure to exercise ordinary care
    C. inability to supervise a large group of students.
    D. reasonable anticipation that an event may occur

B. Negligence is the failure to exercise ordinary or reasonable care.

14. Which item should always be used when using chemicals with noxious vapors?

   A. eye protection
   B. face shield
   C. fume hood
   D. lab apron

C. Fume hoods are designed to protect the experimenter from chemical fumes. The three other choices do not prevent chemical fumes from entering the respiratory system.

15. Identify the correct sequence of organization of living things.

   A. cell – organelle – organ system – tissue – organ – organism
   B. cell – tissue – organ – organ system – organelle – organism
   C. organelle – cell – tissue – organ – organ system – organism
   D. tissue – organelle – organ – cell – organism – organ system

C. An organism, such as a human, is comprised of several organ systems such as the circulatory and nervous systems. These organ systems consist of many organs including the heart and the brain. These organs are made of tissue such as cardiac muscle. Tissues are made up of cells, which contain organelles like the mitochondria and the Golgi apparatus.

16. Which is not a characteristic of living things?

   A. movement
   B. cellular structure
   C. metabolism
   D. reproduction

A. Movement is not a characteristic of life. Viruses are considered non-living organisms but have the ability to move from cell to cell in its host organism.

17. Which kingdom is comprised of organisms made of one cell with no nuclear membrane?

   A. Monera
   B. Protista
   C. Fungi
   D. Algae

A. Monera is the only kingdom that is made up of unicellular organisms with no nucleus. Algae is a protest because it is made up of one type of tissue and it has a nucleus.

18. Potassium chloride is an example of a(n)

   A. non polar covalent bond
   B. polar covalent bond
   C. ionic bond
   D. hydrogen bond

C. Ionic bonds are formed when one electron is stripped away from its atom to join another atom. Ionic compounds are called salts and potassium chloride is a salt; therefore, potassium chloride is an example of an ionic bond.

19. Which of the following is a monomer?

   A. RNA
   B. glycogen
   C. DNA
   D. amino acid

D. A monomer is the simplest unit of structure for a particular macromolecule. Amino acids are the basic unit that comprises a protein. RNA and DNA are polymers consisting of nucleotides and glycogen is a polymer consisting of many molecules of glucose.

20. Which of the following are properties of water?

   I. High specific heat
   II. Strong ionic bonds
   III. Good solvent
   IV. High freezing point

   A. I, III, IV
   B. II and III
   C. I and II
   D. II, III, IV

A. All are properties of water except strong ionic bonds. Water is held together by polar covalent bonds between hydrogen and oxygen.

21. Which does not affect enzyme rate?

   A. increase of temperature
   B. amount of substrate
   C. pH
   D. size of the cell

D. Temperature and pH can affect the rate of reaction of an enzyme. The amount of substrate affects the enzyme as well. The enzyme acts on the substrate. The more substrate, the slower the enzyme rate. Therefore, the only chance left is D, the size of the cell, which has no effect on enzyme rate.

22. Sulfur oxides and nitrogen oxides in the environment react with water to cause

   A. ammonia
   B. acidic precipitation
   C. sulfuric acid
   D. global warming

B. Acidic precipitation is rain, snow, or fog with a pH less than 5.6. It is caused by sulfur oxides and nitrogen oxides that react with water in the air to form acids that fall down to Earth as precipitation.

23. The loss of an electron is _____ and the gain of an electron is _____.

   A. oxidation, reduction
   B. reduction, oxidation
   C. glycolysis, photosynthesis
   D. photosynthesis, glycolysis

A. Oxidation-reduction reactions are also known as redox reactions. In respiration, energy is released by the transfer of electrons by this process. The oxidation phase of this reaction is the loss of an electron and the reduction phase is the gain of an electron.

24. The product of anaerobic respiration in animals is

   A. carbon dioxide
   B. lactic acid
   C. pyruvate
   D. ethyl alcohol

B. In anaerobic lactic acid fermentation, pyruvate is reduced by NADH to form lactic acid. This is the anaerobic process in animals. Alcoholic fermentation is the anaerobic process in yeast and some bacteria resulting in ethyl alcohol. Carbon dioxide and pyruvate are the products of aerobic respiration.

25. In the comparison of respiration to photosynthesis, which statement is true?

   A. oxygen is a waste product in photosynthesis but not in respiration
   B. glucose is produced in respiration but not in photosynthesis
   C. carbon dioxide is formed in photosynthesis but not in respiration
   D. water is formed in respiration but not in photosynthesis

A. In photosynthesis, water is split and the oxygen is given off as a waste product. In respiration, water and carbon dioxide are the waste products.

26. Carbon dioxide is fixed in the form of glucose in

   A. Krebs cycle
   B. the light reactions
   C. the dark reactions (Calvin cycle)
   D. glycolysis

C. The ATP produced during the light reaction is needed to convert carbon dioxide to glucose in the Calvin cycle.

TEACHER CERTIFICATION STUDY GUIDE

27. During the Kreb's cycle, 8 carrier molecules are formed. What are they?

   A. 3 NADH, 3 FADH, 2 ATP
   B. 6 NADH and 2 ATP
   C. 4 FADH$_2$ and 4 ATP
   D. 6 NADH and 2 FADH$_2$

D. For each molecule of CoA that enters the Kreb's cycle, you get 3 NADH and 1 FADH$_2$. There are 2 molecules of CoA so the total yield is 6 NADH and 2 FADH$_2$ during the Kreb's cycle.

28. Which of the following is not posttranscriptional processing?

   A. 5' capping
   B. intron splicing
   C. polypeptide splicing
   D. 3' polyadenylation

C. The removal of segments of polypeptides is a posttranslational process. The other three are methods of posttranscriptional processing.

29. **Polymerase chain reaction**

   A. is a group of polymerases
   B. technique for amplifying DNA
   C. primer for DNA synthesis
   D. synthesis of polymerase

B. PCR is a technique in which a piece of DNA can be amplified into billions of copies within a few hours.

30. **Homozygous individuals**

   A. have two different alleles
   B. are of the same species
   C. have the same features
   D. have a pair of identical alleles

D. Homozygous individuals have a pair of identical alleles and heterozygous individuals have two different alleles.

TEACHER CERTIFICATION STUDY GUIDE

31. The two major ways to determine taxonomic classification are

    A. evolution and phylogeny
    B. reproductive success and evolution
    C. phylogeny and morphology
    D. size and color

C. Taxonomy is based on structure (morphology) and evolutionary relationships (phylogeny).

32. Man's scientific name is Homo sapiens. Choose the proper classification beginning with kingdom and ending with order.

    A. Animalia, Vertebrata, Mammalia, Primate, Hominidae
    B. Animalia, Vertebrata, Chordata, Mammalia, Primate
    C. Animalia, Chordata, Vertebrata, Mammalia, Primate
    D. Chordata, Vertebrata, Primate, Homo, sapiens

C. The order of classification for humans is as follows: Kingdom, Animalia; Phylum, Chordata; Subphylum, Vertebrata; Class, Mammalia; Order, Primate; Family, Hominadae; Genus, Homo; Species, sapiens.

33. The scientific name Canis familiaris refers to the animal's

    A. kingdom and phylum names
    B. genus and species names
    C. class and species names
    D. order and family names

B. Each species is scientifically known by a two-part name, or binomial. The first word in the name is the genus and the second word is its specific epithet (species name).

34. Members of the same species

    A. look identical
    B. never change
    C. reproduce successfully among their group
    D. live in the same geographic location

C. Species are defined by the ability to successfully reproduce with members of their own kind.

BIOLOGICAL SCIENCES

35. What is necessary for diffusion to occur?

   A. carrier proteins
   B. energy
   C. a concentration gradient
   D. a membrane

C. Diffusion is the ability of molecules to move from areas of high concentration to areas of low concentration (a concentration gradient).

36. Which is an example of the use of energy to move a substance through a membrane from areas of low concentration to areas of high concentration?

   A. osmosis
   B. active transport
   C. exocytosis
   D. phagocytosis

B. Active transport can move substances with or against the concentration gradient. This energy requiring process allows for molecules to move from areas of low concentration to high concentration areas.

37. A plant cell is placed in salt water. The resulting movement of water out of the cell is called

   A. facilitated diffusion
   B. diffusion
   C. transpiration
   D. osmosis

D. Osmosis is simply the diffusion of water across a semi-permeable membrane. Water will diffuse out of the cell if there is less water on the outside of the cell.

38. As the amount of waste production increases in a cell, the rate of excretion

   A. slowly decreases
   B. remains the same
   C. increases
   D. stops due to cell death

C. Homeostasis is the control of the differences between internal and external environments. Excretion is the homeostatic system that regulates the amount of waste in a cell. As the amount of waste increases, the rate of excretion will increase to maintain homeostasis.

TEACHER CERTIFICATION STUDY GUIDE

39. A type of molecule not found in the membrane of an animal cell is

    A. phospholipid
    B. protein
    C. cellulose
    D. cholesterol

C. Phospholipids, protein, and cholesterol are all found in animal cells. Cellulose, however, is only found in plant cells.

40. Which type of cell would contain the most mitochondria?

    A. muscle cell
    B. nerve cell
    C. epithelium
    D. blood cell

A. Mitochondria are the site of cellular respiration where ATP is made. Muscle cells have the most mitochondria because they use a great deal of energy.

41. The first cells that evolved on earth were probably of which type?

    A. autotrophs
    B. eukaryotes
    C. heterotrophs
    D. prokaryotes

D. Prokaryotes date back to 3.5 billion years ago in the first fossil record. Their ability to adapt to the environment allows them to thrive in a wide variety of habitats.

42. According to the fluid-mosaic model of the cell membrane, membranes are composed of

    A. phospholipid bilayers with proteins embedded in the layers
    B. one layer of phospholipids with cholesterol embedded in the layer
    C. two layers of protein with lipids embedded the layers
    D. DNA and fluid proteins

A. Cell membranes are composed of two phospholipids with their hydrophobic tails sandwiched between their hydrophilic heads, creating a lipid bilayer. The membrane contains proteins embedded in the layer (integral proteins) and proteins on the surface (peripheral proteins).

43. All the following statements regarding both a mitochondria and a chloroplast are correct except

   A. they both produce energy over a gradient
   B. they both have DNA and are capable of reproduction
   C. they both transfer light energy to chemical energy
   D. they both make ATP

C. Cellular respiration does not transfer light energy to chemical energy. Cellular respiration transfers electrons to release energy. Photosynthesis utilizes light energy to produce chemical energy.

44. This stage of mitosis includes cytokinesis or division of the cytoplasm and its organelles

   A. anaphase
   B. interphase
   C. prophase
   D. telophase

D. The last stage of the mitotic phase is telophase. Here, the two nuclei form with a full set of DNA each. The cell is pinched into two cells and cytokinesis, or division of the cytoplasm and organelles, occurs.

45. Replication of chromosomes occurs during which phase of the cell cycle?

   A. prophase
   B. interphase
   C. metaphase
   D. anaphase

B. Interphase is the stage where the cell grows and copies the chromosomes in preparation for the mitotic phase.

46. Which statement regarding mitosis is correct?

   A. diploid cells produce haploid cells for sexual reproduction
   B. sperm and egg cells are produced
   C. diploid cells produce diploid cells for growth and repair
   D. it allows for greater genetic diversity

C. The purpose of mitotic cell division is to provide growth and repair in body (somatic) cells. The cells begin as diploid and produce diploid cells.

47. In a plant cell, telophase is described as

   A. the time of chromosome doubling
   B. cell plate formation
   C. the time when crossing over occurs
   D. cleavage furrow formation

B. During plant cell telophase, a cell plate is observed whereas a cleavage furrow is formed in animal cells.

48. Identify this stage of mitosis

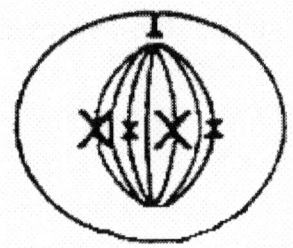

   A. anaphase
   B. metaphase
   C. telophase
   D. prophase

B. During metaphase, the centromeres are at opposite ends of the cell. Here the chromosomes are aligned with one another.

49. Identify this stage of mitosis

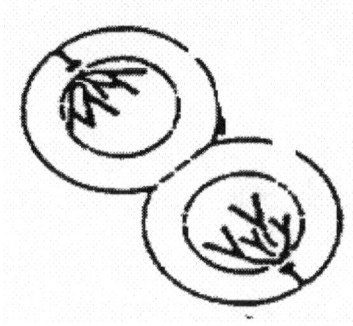

- A. prophase
- B. telophase
- C. anaphase
- D. metaphase

B. Telophase is the last stage of mitosis. Here, two nuclei become visible and the nuclear membrane resembles.

50. Identify this stage of mitosis

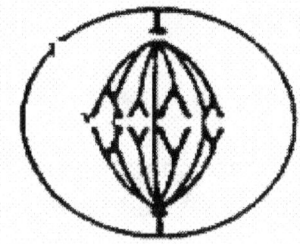

- A. anaphase
- B. metaphase
- C. prophase
- D. telophase

A. During anaphase, the centromeres split in half and homologous chromosomes separate.

51. Oxygen is given off in the

   A. light reactions of photosynthesis
   B. dark reactions of photosynthesis
   C. Krebs cycle
   D. reduction of NAD+ to NADH

A. The conversion of solar energy to chemical energy occurs in the light reactions. Electrons are transferred by the absorption of light by chlorophyll and causes water to split, releasing oxygen as a waste product.

52. In the electron transport chain, all the following are true except

   A. it occurs in the mitochondrion
   B. it does not make ATP directly
   C. the net gain of energy is 30 ATP
   D. most molecules in the electron transport chain are proteins.

C. The end result of the electron transport chain is 34 molecules of ATP.

53. The area of a DNA nucleotide that varies is the

   A. deoxyribose
   B. phosphate group
   C. nitrogen base
   D. sugar

C. DNA is made of a 5 carbon sugar (deoxyribose), a phosphate group, and a nitrogenous base. There are four nitrogenous bases in DNA that allow for the four different nucleotides.

54. A DNA strand has the base sequence of TCAGTA. Its DNA complement would have the following sequence

   A. ATGACT
   B. TCAGTA
   C. AGUCAU
   D. AGTCAT

D. The complement strand to a single strand DNA molecule has a complementary sequence to the template strand. T pairs with A and C pairs with G. Therefore, the complement to TCAGTA is AGTCAT.

TEACHER CERTIFICATION STUDY GUIDE

55. Genes function in specifying the structure of which molecule?

   A. carbohydrates
   B. lipids
   C. nucleic acids
   D. proteins

D. Genes contain the sequence of nucleotides that code for amino acids. Amino acids are the building blocks of protein.

56. What is the correct order of steps in protein synthesis?

   A. transcription, then replication
   B. transcription, then translation
   C. translation, then transcription
   D. replication, then translation

B. A DNA strand first undergoes transcription to get a complementary mRNA strand. Translation of the mRNA strand then occurs to result in the tRNA adding the appropriate amino acid for an ending product of a protein.

57. This carries amino acids to the ribosome in protein synthesis

   A. messenger RNA
   B. ribosomal RNA
   C. transfer RNA
   D. DNA

C. The tRNA molecule is specific for a particular amino acid. The tRNA has an anticodon sequence that is complementary to the codon. This specifies where the tRNA places the amino acid in protein synthesis.

58. A protein is sixty amino acids in length. This requires a coded DNA sequence of how many nucleotides?

   A. 20
   B. 30
   C. 120
   D. 180

D. Each amino acid codon consists of 3 nucleotides. If there are 60 amino acids in a protein, then 60 x 30 = 180 nucleotides.

BIOLOGICAL SCIENCES

59. A DNA molecule has the sequence of ACTATG. What is the anticodon of this molecule?

A. UGAUAC
B. ACUAUG
C. TGATAC
D. ACTATG

B. The DNA is first transcribed into mRNA. Here, the DNA has the sequence ACTATG; therefore the complementary mRNA sequence is UGAUAC (remember, in RNA, T are U). This mRNA sequence is the codon. The anticodon is the complement to the codon. The anticodon sequence will be ACUAUG (remember, the anticodon is tRNA, so U is present instead of T).

60. The term "phenotype" refers to which of the following?

A. a condition which is heterozygous
B. the genetic makeup of an individual
C. a condition which is homozygous
D. how the genotype is expressed

D. Phenotype is the physical appearance of an organism due to its genetic makeup (genotype).

61. The ratio of brown-eyed to blue-eyed children from the mating of a blue-eyed male to a heterozygous brown-eyed female would be expected to be which of the following?

A. 2:1
B. 1:1
C. 1:0
D. 1:2

B. Use a Punnet square to determine the ratio.

	b	b
B	Bb	Bb
b	bb	bb

B = brown eyes, b = blue eyes

Female genotype is on the side and the male genotype is across the top.

The female is heterozygous and her phenotype is brown eyes. This means the dominant allele is for brown eyes. The male expresses the homozygous recessive allele for blue eyes. Their children are expected to have a ratio of brown eyes to blue eyes of 2:2; or 1:1.

62. The Law of Segregation defined by Mendel states that

   A. when sex cells form, the two alleles that determine a trait will end up on different gametes
   B. only one of two alleles is expressed in a heterozygous organism
   C. the allele expressed is the dominant allele
   D. alleles of one trait do not affect the inheritance of alleles on another chromosome

A. The law of segregation states that the two alleles for each trait segregate into different gametes.

63. When a white flower is crossed with a red flower, incomplete dominance can be seen by the production of which of the following?

   A. pink flowers
   B. red flowers
   C. white flowers
   D. red and white flowers

A. Incomplete dominance is when the F_1 generation results in an appearance somewhere between the parents. Red flowers crossed with white flowers results in an F_1 generation with pink flowers.

64. Sutton observed that genes and chromosomes behaved the same. This led him to his theory which stated

   A. that meiosis causes chromosome separation
   B. that linked genes are able to separate
   C. that genes and chromosomes have the same function
   D. that genes are found on chromosomes

D. Sutton observed how mitosis and meiosis confirmed Mendel's theory on "factors." His Chromosome Theory states that genes are located on chromosomes.

65. Amniocentesis is

   A. a non-invasive technique for detecting genetic disorders
   B. a bacterial infection
   C. extraction of amniotic fluid
   D. removal of fetal tissue

C. Amniocentesis is a procedure in which a needle is inserted into the uterus to extract some of the amniotic fluid surrounding the fetus. Some genetic disorders can be detected by chemicals in the fluid.

66. A child with type O blood has a father with type A blood and a mother with type B blood. The genotypes of the parents respectively would be which of the following?

   A. AA and BO
   B. AO and BO
   C. AA and BB
   D. AO and OO

B. Type O blood has 2 recessive O genes. A child receives one allele from each parent; therefore each parent in this example must have an O allele. The father has type A blood with a genotype of AO and the mother has type B blood with a genotype of BO.

67. Any change that affects the sequence of bases in a gene is called a(n)

   A. deletion
   B. polyploid
   C. mutation
   D. duplication

C. A mutation is an inheritable change in DNA. They may be errors in replication or a spontaneous rearrangement of one ore more segments of DNA. Deletion and duplication are type of mutations. Polyploidy is when and organism has more than two complete chromosome sets.

68. The *lac* operon

   I. contains the *lac Z, lac Y, lac A* genes
   II. converts glucose to lactose
   III. contains a repressor
   IV. is on when the repressor is activated

   A. I
   B. II
   C. III and IV
   D. I and III

D. The *lac* operon contains the genes that encode for the enzymes used to convert lactose into fuel. It contains three genes: *lac A, lac Z,* and *lac Y.* It also contains a promoter and repressor. When the repressor is activated, the operon is off.

TEACHER CERTIFICATION STUDY GUIDE

69. **Which of the following factors will affect the Hardy-Weinberg law of equilibrium, leading to evolutionary change?**

    A. no mutations
    B. non-random mating
    C. no immigration or emigration
    D. Large population

B. There are five requirements to keep the Hardy-Weinberg equilibrium stable: no mutation, no selection pressures, an isolated population, a large population, and random mating.

70. **If a population is in Hardy-Weinberg equilibrium and the frequency of the recessive allele is 0.3, what percentage of the population would be expected to be heterozygous?**

    A. 9%
    B. 49%
    C. 42%
    D. 21%

C. 0.3 is the value of q. Therefore, $q^2 = 0.09$. According to the Hardy-Weinberg equation, $1 = p + q$.

$1 = p + 0.3$.
$p = 0.7$
$p^2 = 0.49$

Next, plug q^2 and p^2 into the equation $1 = p^2 + 2pq + q^2$.

$1 = 0.49 + 2pq + 0.09$ (where 2pq is the number of heterozygotes).
$1 = 0.58 + 2pq$
$2pq = 0.42$

Multiply by 100 to get the percent of heterozygotes to get 42%.

BIOLOGICAL SCIENCES

71. **Crossing over, which increases genetic diversity, occurs during which stage(s)?**

    A. telophase II in meiosis
    B. metaphase in mitosis
    C. interphase in both mitosis and meiosis
    D. prophase I in meiosis

D. During prophase I of meiosis, the replicated chromosomes condense and pair with homologues in a process called synapsis. Crossing over, the exchange of genetic material between homologues to further increase diversity, occurs during prophase I.

72. **Cancer cells divide extensively and invade other tissues. This continuous cell division is due to**

    A. density dependent inhibition
    B. density independent inhibition
    C. chromosome replication
    D. Growth factors

B. Density dependent inhibition is when the cells crowd one another and consume all the nutrients; therefore halting cell division. Cancer cells, however, are density independent; meaning they can divide continuously as long as nutrients are present.

73. **Which process(es) results in a haploid chromosome number?**

    A. both meiosis and mitosis
    B. mitosis
    C. meiosis
    D. replication and division

C. In meiosis, there are two consecutive cell divisions resulting in the reduction of the chromosome number by half (diploid to haploid).

74. **Segments of DNA can be transferred from the DNA of one organism to another through the use of which of the following?**

    A. bacterial plasmids
    B. viruses
    C. chromosomes from frogs
    D. plant DNA

A. Plasmids can transfer themselves (and therefore their genetic information) by a process called conjugation. This requires cell-cell contact.

75. Which of the following is not true regarding restriction enzymes?

A. they do not aid in recombination procedures
B. they are used in genetic engineering
C. they are named after the bacteria in which they naturally occur
D. they identify and splice certain base sequences on DNA

A. A restriction enzyme is a bacterial enzyme that cuts foreign DNA at specific locations. The splicing of restriction fragments into a plasmid results in a recombinant plasmid.

76. A virus that can remain dormant until a certain environmental condition causes its rapid increase is said to be

A. lytic
B. benign
C. saprophytic
D. lysogenic

D. Lysogenic viruses remain dormant until something initiates it to break out of the host cell.

77. Which is not considered to be a morphological type of bacteria?

A. obligate
B. coccus
C. spirillum
D. bacillus

A. Morphology is the shape of an organism. Obligate is term used when describing dependence on something. Coccus is a round bacterium, spirillum is a spiral shaped bacterium, and bacillus is a rod shaped bacterium.

78. Antibiotics are effective in fighting bacterial infections due to their ability to

A. interfere with DNA replication in the bacteria
B. prevent the formation of new cell walls in the bacteria
C. disrupt the ribosome of the bacteria
D. All of the above.

D. Antibiotics can destroy the bacterial cell wall, interfere with bacterial DNA replication, and disrupt the bacterial ribosome without affecting the host cells.

79. Bacteria commonly reproduce by a process called binary fission. Which of the following best defines this process?

    A. viral vectors carry DNA to new bacteria
    B. DNA from one bacterium enters another
    C. DNA doubles and the bacterial cell divides
    D. DNA from dead cells is absorbed into bacteria

C. Binary fission is the asexual process in which the bacteria divide in half after the DNA doubles. This results in an exact clone of the parent cell.

80. All of the following are examples of a member of Kingdom Fungi except

    A. mold
    B. algae
    C. mildew
    D. mushrooms

B. Mold, mildew, and mushrooms are all fungi. Brown algae and golden algae are members of the kingdom protista and green algae are members of the plant kingdom.

81. Protists are classified into major groups according to

    A. their method of obtaining nutrition
    B. reproduction
    C. metabolism
    D. their form and function

D. The chaotic status of names and concepts of the higher classification of the protists reflects their great diversity in form, function, and life styles. The protists are often grouped as algae (plant-like), protozoa (animal-like), or fungus-like based on the similarity of their lifestyle and characteristics to these more derived groups.

82. In comparison to protist cells, moneran cells

   I. are usually smaller
   II. evolved later
   III. are more complex
   IV. contain more organelles

   A. I
   B. I and II
   C. II and III
   D. I and IV

A. Moneran cells are almost always smaller than protists. Moneran cells are prokaryotic; therefore they are less complex and have no organelles. Prokaryotes were the first cells on Earth and therefore evolved before than the eukaryotic protists.

83. Spores characterize the reproduction mode for which of the following group of plants?

   A. algae
   B. flowering plants
   C. conifers
   D. ferns

D. Ferns are non-seeded vascular plants. All plants in this group have spores and require water for reproduction. Algae, flowering plants, and conifers are not in this group of plants.

84. Water movement to the top of a twenty foot tree is most likely due to which principle?

   A. osmostic pressure
   B. xylem pressure
   C. capillarity
   D. transpiration

D. Xylem is the tissue that transports water upward. Transpiration is the force that pulls the water upwards. Transpiration is the evaporation of water from leaves.

85. What are the stages of development from the egg to the plant?

   A. morphogenesis, growth, and cellular differentiation
   B. cell differentiation, growth, and morphogenesis
   C. growth, morphogenesis, and cellular differentiation
   D. growth, cellular differentiation, and morphogensis

C. The development of the egg to form a plant occurs in three stages: growth; morphogenesis, the development of form; and cellular differentiation, the acquisition of a cell's specific structure and function.

86. In angiosperms, the food for the developing plant is found in which of the following structures?

   A. ovule
   B. endosperm
   C. male gametophyte
   D. cotyledon

B. The endosperm is a product of double fertilization. It is the food supply for the developing plant.

87. The process in which pollen grains are released from the anthers is called

   A. pollination
   B. fertilization
   C. blooming
   D. dispersal

A. Pollen grains are released from the anthers during pollination and carried by animals and the wind to land on the carpels.

TEACHER CERTIFICATION STUDY GUIDE

88. Which of the following is not a characteristic of a monocot?

   A. parallel veins in leaves
   B. petals of flowers occur in multiples of 4 or 5
   C. one seed leaf
   D. vascular tissue scattered throughout the stem

B. Monocots have one cotelydon, parallel veins in their leaves, and their flower petals are in multiples of threes. Dicots have flower petals in multiples of fours and fives.

89. What controls gas exchange on the bottom of a plant leaf?

   A. stomata
   B. epidermis
   C. collenchyma and schlerenchyma
   D. palisade mesophyll

A. Stomata provide openings on the underside of leaves for oxygen to move in or out of the plant and for carbon dioxide to move in.

90. How are angiosperms different from other groups of plants?

   A. presence of flowers and fruits
   B. production of spores for reproduction
   C. true roots and stems
   D. seed production

A. Angiosperms do not have spores for reproduction. They do have true roots and stems as do all vascular plants. They do have seed production as do the gymnosperms. The presence of flowers and fruits is the difference between angiosperms and other plants.

91. Generations of plants alternate between

   A. angiosperms and bryophytes
   B. flowering and nonflowering stages
   C. seed bearing and spore bearing plants
   D. haploid and diploid stages

D. Reproduction of plants is accomplished through alteration of generations. Simply stated, a haploid stage in the plant's life history alternates with a diploid stage.

BIOLOGICAL SCIENCES

92. Double fertilization refers to which choice of the following?

   A. two sperm fertilizing one egg
   B. fertilization of a plant by gametes from two separate plants
   C. two sperm enter the plant embryo sac; one sperm fertilizes the egg, the other forms the endosperm
   D. the production of non-identical twins through fertilization of two separate eggs

C. In angiosperms, double fertilization is when an ovum is fertilized by two sperm. One sperm produces the new plant and the other forms the food supply for the developing plant (endosperm).

93. Characteristics of coelomates include:

   I. no true digestive system
   II. two germ layers
   III. true fluid filled cavity
   IV. three germ layers

   A. I
   B. II and IV
   C. IV
   D. III and IV

D. Coelomates are triplobastic animals (3 germ layers). They have a true fluid filled body cavity called a coelom.

94. Which phylum accounts for 85% of all animal species?

   A. Nematoda
   B. Chordata
   C. Arthropoda
   D. Cnidaria

C. The arthropoda phylum consists of insects, crustaceans, and spiders. They are the largest group in the animal kingdom.

95. Which is the correct statement regarding the human nervous system and the human endocrine system?

   A. the nervous system maintains homeostasis whereas the endocrine system does not
   B. endocrine glands produce neurotransmitters whereas nerves produce hormones
   C. nerve signals travel on neurons whereas hormones travel through the blood
   D. he nervous system involves chemical transmission whereas the endocrine system does not

C. In the human nervous system, neurons carry nerve signals to and from the cell body. Endocrine glands produce hormones that are carried through the body in the bloodstream.

96. A muscular adaptation to move food through the digestive system is called

   A. peristalsis
   B. passive transport
   C. voluntary action
   D. bulk transport

A. Peristalsis is a process of wave-like contractions. This process allows food to be carried down the pharynx and though the digestive tract.

97. The role of neurotransmitters in nerve action is

   A. turn off sodium pump
   B. turn off calcium pump
   C. send impulse to neuron
   D. send impulse to the body

A. The neurotransmitters turn off the sodium pump which results in depolarization of the membrane.

98. Fats are broken down by which substance?

   A. bile produced in the gall bladder
   B. lipase produced in the gall bladder
   C. glucagons produced in the liver
   D. bile produced in the liver

D. The liver produces bile which breaks down and emulsifies fatty acids.

BIOLOGICAL SCIENCES

99. Fertilization in humans usually occurs in the

A. uterus
B. ovary
C. fallopian tubes
D. vagina

C. Fertilization of the egg by the sperm normally occurs in the fallopian tube. The fertilized egg is then implanted on the uterine lining for development.

100. All of the following are found in the dermis layer of skin except

A. sweat glands
B. keratin
C. hair follicles
D. blood vessels

B. Keratin is a water proofing protein found in the epidermis.

101. Which is the correct sequence of embryonic development in a frog?

A. cleavage – blastula – gastrula
B. cleavage – gastrula – blastula
C. blastula – cleavage – gastrula
D. gastrula – blastula – cleavage

A. Animals go through several stages of development after fertilization of the egg cell. The first step is cleavage which continues until the egg becomes a blastula. The blastula is a hollow ball of undifferentiated cells. Gastrulation is the next step. This is the time of tissue differentiation into the separate germ layers: the endoderm, mesoderm, and ectoderm.

102. Food is carried through the digestive tract by a series of wave-like contractions. This process is called

A. peristalsis
B. chyme
C. digestion
D. absorption

A. Peristalsis is the process of wave-like contractions that moves food through the digestive tract.

103. Movement is possible by the action of muscles pulling on

A. skin
B. bones
C. joints
D. ligaments

B. The muscular system's function is for movement. Skeletal muscles are attached to bones and are responsible for their movement.

104. All of the following are functions of the skin except

A. storage
B. protection
C. sensation
D. regulation of temperature

A. Skin is a protective barrier against infection. It contains hair follicles that respond to sensation and it plays a role in thermoregulation.

105. Hormones are essential to the regulation of reproduction. What organ is responsible for the release of hormones for sexual maturity?

A. pituitary gland
B. hypothalamus
C. pancreas
D. thyroid gland

B. The hypothalamus begins secreting hormones that help mature the reproductive system and development of the secondary sex characteristics.

106. A bicyclist has a heart rate of 110 beats per minute and a stroke volume of 85 mL per beat. What is the cardiac output?

A. 9.35 L/min
B. 1.29 L/min
C. 0.772 L/min
D. 129 L/min

A. The cardiac output is the volume of blood per minute that is pumped into the systemic circuit. This is determined by the heart rate and the stroke volume. Multiply the heart rate by the stroke volume. 110 * 85 = 9350 mL/min. Divide by 1000 to get units of liters. 9350/1000 = 9.35 L/min.

107. After sea turtles are hatched on the beach, they start the journey to the ocean. This is due to

    A. innate behavior
    B. territoriality
    C. the tide
    D. learned behavior

A. Innate behavior are inborn or instinctual. The baby sea turtles did not learn from their mother. They immediately knew to head towards the ocean once they hatched.

108. A school age boy had the chicken pox as a baby. He will most likely not get this disease again because of

    A. passive immunity
    B. vaccination
    C. antibiotics
    D. active immunity

D. Active immunity develops after recovery from an infectious disease, such as the chicken pox, or after vaccination. Passive immunity may be passed from one individual to another (from mother to nursing child).

109. High humidity and temperature stability are present in which of the following biomes?

    A. taiga
    B. deciduous forest
    C. desert
    D. tropical rain forest

D. A tropical rain forest is located near the equator. Its temperature is at a constant 25 degrees C and the humidity is high due to the rainfall that exceeds 200 cm per year.

110. The biological species concept applies to

A. asexual organisms
B. extinct organisms
C. sexual organisms
D. fossil organisms

C. The biological species concept states that a species is a reproductive community of populations that occupy a specific niche in nature. It focuses on reproductive isolation of populations as the primary criterion for recognition of species status. The biological species concept does not apply to organisms that are completely asexual in their reproduction, fossil organisms, or distinctive populations that hybridize.

111. Which term is not associated with the water cycle?

A. precipitation
B. transpiration
C. fixation
D. evaporation

C. Water is recycled through the processes of evaporation and precipitation. Transpiration is the evaporation of water from leaves. Fixation is not associated with the water cycle.

112. All of the following are density independent factors that affect a population except

A. temperature
B. rainfall
C. predation
D. soil nutrients

C. As a population increases, the competition for resources is intense and the growth rate declines. This is a density-dependent factor. An example of this would be predation. Density-independent factors affect the population regardless of its size. Examples of density-independent factors are rainfall, temperature, and soil nutrients.

113. In the growth of a population, the increase is exponential until carrying capacity is reached. This is represented by a (n)

- A. S curve
- B. J curve
- C. M curve
- D. L curve

A. An exponentially growing population starts off with little change and then rapidly increases. The graphic representation of this growth curve has the appearance of a "J". However, as the carrying capacity of the exponentially growing population is reached, the growth rate begins to slow down and level off. The graphic representation of this growth curve has the appearance of an "S".

114. Primary succession occurs after

- A. nutrient enrichment
- B. a forest fire
- C. bare rock is exposed after a water table recedes
- D. a housing development is built

C. Primary succession occurs where life never existed before, such as flooded areas or a new volcanic island. It is only after the water recedes that the rock is able to support new life.

115. Crabgrass – grasshopper – frog – snake – eagle. If DDT were present in an ecosystem, which organism would have the highest concentration in its system?

- A. grasshopper
- B. eagle
- C. frog
- D. crabgrass

B. Chemicals and pesticides accumulate along the food chain. Tertiary consumers have more accumulated toxins than animals at the bottom of the food chain.

116. Which trophic level has the highest ecological efficiency?

A. decomposers
B. producers
C. tertiary consumers
D. secondary consumers

B. The amount of energy that is transferred between trophic levels is called the ecological efficiency. The visual of this is represented in a pyramid of productivity. The producers have the greatest amount of energy and are at the bottom of this pyramid.

117. A clownfish is protected by the sea anemone's tentacles. In turn, the anemone receives uneaten food from the clownfish. This is an example of

A. mutualism
B. parasitism
C. commensalisms
D. competition

A. Neither the clownfish nor the anemone cause harmful effects towards one another and they both benefit from their relationship. Mutualism is when two species that occupy a similar space benefit from their relationship.

118. If the niches of two species overlap, what usually results?

A. a symbiotic relationship
B. cooperation
C. competition
D. a new species

C. Two species that occupy the same habitat or eat the same food are said to be in competition with each other.

119. Oxygen created in photosynthesis comes from the breakdown of

A. carbon dioxide
B. water
C. glucose
D. carbon monoxide

B. In photosynthesis, water is split; the hydrogen atoms are pulled to carbon dioxide which is taken in by the plant and ultimately reduced to make glucose. The oxygen from the water is given off as a waste product.

120. Which photosystem makes ATP?

A. photosystem I
B. photosystem II
C. photosystem III
D. photosystem IV

A. Photosystem I is composed of a pair of chlorophyll *a* molecules It makes ATP whose energy is needed to build glucose.

121. All of the following gasses made up the primitive atmosphere except

A. ammonia
B. methane
C. oxygen
D. hydrogen

C. In the 1920s, Oparin and Haldane were to first to theorize that the primitive atmosphere was a reducing atmosphere with no oxygen. The gases were rich in hydrogen, methane, water, and ammonia.

122. The Endosymbiotic theory states that

A. eukaryotes arose from prokaryotes
B. animals evolved in close relationships with one another
C. the prokaryotes arose from eukaryotes
D. life arose from inorganic compounds

A. The Endosymbiotic theory of the origin of eukaryotes states that eukaryotes arose from symbiotic groups of prokaryotic cells. According to this theory, smaller prokaryotes lived within larger prokaryotic cells, eventually evolving into chloroplasts and mitochondria.

123. Which aspect of science does not support evolution?

A. comparative anatomy
B. organic chemistry
C. comparison of DNA among organisms
D. analogous structures

B. Comparative anatomy is the comparison of characteristics of the anatomies of different species. This includes homologous structures and analogous structures. The comparison of DNA between species is the best known way to place species on the evolution tree. Organic chemistry has nothing to do with evolution.

124. Evolution occurs in

A. individuals
B. populations
C. organ systems
D. cells

B. Evolution is a change in genotype over time. Gene frequencies shift and change from generation to generation. Populations evolve, not individuals.

125. Which process contributes to the large variety of living things in the world today?

A. meiosis
B. asexual reproduction
C. mitosis
D. alternation of generations

A. During meiosis prophase I crossing over occurs. This exchange of genetic material between homologues increases diversity.

126. The wing of bird, human arm and whale flipper have the same bone structure. These are called

A. polymorphic structures
B. homologous structures
C. vestigial structures
D. analogous structures

B. Homologous characteristics have the same genetic basis (leading to similar appearances) but are used for a different function.

127. Which biome is the most prevalent on Earth?

A. marine
B. desert
C. savanna
D. tundra

A. The marine biome covers 75% of the Earth. This biome is organized by the depth of water.

128. Which of the following is not an abiotic factor?

- A. temperature
- B. rainfall
- C. soil quality
- D. bacteria

D. Abiotic factors are non-living aspects of an ecosystem. Bacteria is an example of a biotic factor—a living thing in an ecosystem.

129. DNA synthesis results in a strand that is synthesized continuously. This is the

- A. lagging strand
- B. leading strand
- C. template strand
- D. complementary strand

B. As DNA synthesis proceeds along the replication fork, one strand is replicated continuously (the leading strand) and the other strand is replicated discontinuously (lagging strand).

130. Using a gram staining technique, it is observed that E. coli stains pink. It is therefore

- A. gram positive
- B. dead
- C. gram negative
- D. gram neutral

C. A Gram positive bacterium absorbs the stain and appears purple under a microscope because of its cell wall made of peptidoglycan. A Gram negative bacterium does not absorb the stain because of its more complex cell wall. These bacteria appear pink under a microscope.

TEACHER CERTIFICATION STUDY GUIDE

131. A light microscope has an ocular of 10X and an objective of 40X. What is the total magnification?

- A. 400X
- B. 30X
- C. 50X
- D. 4000X

A. To determine the total magnification of a microscope, multiply the ocular lens by the objective lens. Here, the ocular lens is 10X and the objective lens is 40X.

(10X) X (40X) = 400X total magnification

132. Three plants were grown. The following data was taken. Determine the mean growth. Plant 1: 10cm Plant 2: 20cm Plant 3: 15cm

- A. 5 cm
- B. 45 cm
- C. 12 cm
- D. 15 cm

D. The mean growth is the average of the three growth heights.

$$\frac{10 + 20 + 15}{3} = 15 \text{cm average height}$$

133. Electrophoresis separates DNA on the basis of

- A. amount of current
- B. molecular size
- C. positive charge of the molecule
- D. solubility of the gel

B. Electrophoresis uses electrical charges of molecules to separate them according to their size.

BIOLOGICAL SCIENCES

134. The reading of a meniscus in a graduated cylinder is done at the

    A. top of the meniscus
    B. middle of the meniscus
    C. bottom of the meniscus
    D. closest whole number

C. The graduated cylinder is the common instrument used for measuring volume. It is important for the accuracy of the measurement to read the volume level of the liquid at the bottom of the meniscus. The meniscus is the curved surface of the liquid.

135. Two hundred plants were grown. Fifty plants died. What percentage of the plants survived?

    A. 40%
    B. 25%
    C. 75%
    D. 50%

C. This is a proportion. If 50 plants died, then 200 – 50 = 150 survived. The number of survivors is the numerator and the total number of plants grown is the denominator.

$$\frac{150}{200} = 0.75 \text{ Multiply by 100 to get percent} = 75\% \text{ survive}$$

136. Which is not a correct statement regarding the use of a light microscope?

    A. carry the microscope with two hands
    B. store on the low power objective
    C. clean all lenses with lens paper
    D. Focus first on high power

D. Always begin focusing on low power. This allows for the observation of microorganisms in a larger field of view. Switch to high power once you have a microorganism in view on low power.

137. Spectrophotometry utilizes the principle of

A. light transmission
B. molecular weight
C. solubility of the substance
D. electrical charges

A. Spectrophotometry uses percent of light at different wavelengths absorbed and transmitted by a pigment solution.

138. Chromotography is most often associated with the separation of

A. nutritional elements
B. DNA
C. proteins
D. plant pigments

D. Chromatography uses the principles of capillarity to separate substances such as plant pigments. Molecules of a larger size will move slower up the paper, whereas smaller molecules will move more quickly producing lines of pigment.

139. A genetic engineering advancement in the medical field is

A. gene therapy
B. pesticides
C. degradation of harmful chemicals
D. antibiotics

A. Gene therapy is the introduction of a normal allele to the somatic cells to replace a defective allele. The medical field has had success in treating patients with a single enzyme deficiency disease. Gene therapy has allowed doctors and scientists to introduce a normal allele that would provide the missing enzyme.

140. Which scientists are credited with the discovery of the structure of DNA?

A. Hershey & Chase
B. Sutton & Morgan
C. Watson & Crick
D. Miller & Fox

C. In the 1950s, James Watson and Francis Crick discovered the structure of a DNA molecule as that of a double helix.

141. Negatively charged particles that circle the nucleus of an atom are called

- A. neutrons
- B. neutrinos
- C. electrons
- D. protons

C. Neutrons and protons make up the core of an atom. Neutrons have no charge and protons are positively charged. Electrons are the negatively charged particles around the nucleus.

142. The shape of a cell depends on its

- A. function
- B. structure
- C. age
- D. size

A. In most living organisms, its structure is based on its function.

143. The most ATP is generated through

- A. fermentation
- B. glycolysis
- C. chemiosmosis
- D. Krebs cycle

C. The electron transport chain uses electrons to pump hydrogen ions across the mitochondrial membrane. This ion gradient is used to form ATP in a process called chemiosmosis. ATP is generated by the movement of hydrogen ions off NADH and $FADH_2$. This yields 34 ATP molecules.

144. In DNA, adenine bonds with ____, while cytosine bonds with ____.

- A. thymine/guanine
- B. adenine/cytosine
- C. cytosine/adenine
- D. guanine/thymine

A. In DNA, adenine pairs with thymine and cytosine pairs with guanine because of their nitrogenous base structures.

145. The individual parts of cells are best studied using a (n)

- A. ultracentrifuge
- B. phase-contrast microscope
- C. CAT scan
- D. electron microscope

D. The scanning electron microscope uses a beam of electrons to pass through the specimen. The resolution is about 1000 times greater than that of a light microscope. This allows the scientist to view extremely small objects, such as the individual parts of a cell.

146. Thermoacidophiles are

- A. prokaryotes
- B. eukaryotes
- C. protists
- D. archaea

D. Thermoacidophiles, methanogens, and halobacteria are members of the archaea group. They are as diverse from prokaryotes as prokaryotes are to eukaryotes.

147. Which of the following is not a type of fiber that makes up the cytoskeleton?

- A. vacuoles
- B. microfilaments
- C. microtubules
- D. intermediate filaments

A. Vacuoles are mostly found in plants and hold stored food and pigments. The other three choices are fibers that make up the cytoskeleton found in both plant and animal cells.

148. Viruses are made of

- A. a protein coat surrounding a nucleic acid
- B. DNA, RNA and a cell wall
- C. a nucleic acid surrounding a protein coat
- D. protein surrounded by DNA

A. Viruses are composed of a protein coat and a nucleic acid; either RNA or DNA.

149. Reproductive isolation results in

   A. extinction
   B. migration
   C. follilization
   D. speciation

D. Reproductive isolation is caused by any factor that impedes two species from producing viable, fertile hybrids. Reproductive isolation of populations is the primary criterion for recognition of species status.

150. This protein structure consists of the coils and folds of polypeptide chains. Which is it?

   A. secondary structure
   B. quaternary structure
   C. tertiary structure
   D. primary structure

A. Primary structure is the protein's unique sequence of amino acids. Secondary structure is the coils and folds of polypeptide chains. The coils and folds are the result of hydrogen bonds along the polypeptide backbone. Tertiary structure is formed by bonding between the side chains of the amino acids. Quaternary structure is the overall structure of the protein from the aggregation of two or more polypeptide chains.

www.ingramcontent.com/pod-product-compliance
Lightning Source LLC
Chambersburg PA
CBHW080539300426
44111CB00017B/2800